Everyday Miracles

Instructor's Guide

By Julia Royston

Edited by: Claude R. Royston

B. K. Royston Publishing, Inc.
Jeffersonville, Indiana

BK Royston Publishing, Inc.
P. O. Box 4321
Jeffersonville, IN 47130
502-802-5385
http://bkroystonpublishing.blogspot.com
www.juliaroyston.com

© 2010 by Julia A. Royston

All rights reserved. No part of this book may be reproduced, stored in a retrieval system, or transmitted by any means without the written permission of the author.

Published by: BK Royston Publishing
Cover design by: Julia A. Royston
Layout by: Julia A. Royston

ISBN-13: 978-09818135-4-7

Clip Art copyright 2010 Microsoft, Inc.

Unless otherwise indicated, all scripture text is from the King James Version of the bible.

Printed in the United States of America

Titles by Julia A. Royston

A New Season in Word: Inspirations for Divine Living
How Hot is Your Love Life: Return to Your First Love.
Revised Edition.
Everyday Miracles

Music by Julia A. Royston

Joy in His Presence
Hymns for Him
A New Season in Word and Song
Begin Again
For Your Glory Lord
Everyday Miracles

All resources available at www.juliaroyston.com

Acknowledgements

I thank my Lord and Savior Jesus Christ for giving me another opportunity for more people to know and fall in love with Him. I thank you that you have entrusted this gift to me. Lord, let your Spirit move through this book to the people who will read it. Father, continue to work miracles in all of our lives.

To my wonderful husband Brian for loving and supporting me so much that I can be and do all that God has designed and purposed.

Thank you to my parents, Dr. Jack & Mrs. Daisy Foree, who unconditionally believe in me and support me in every project.

A special thank you to Rev. Claude R. Royston for using his wisdom and spiritual insight to edit this book. Special thank you to Mrs. Lillie Royston for your support, love and being the best sales manager ever.

Table of Contents

Alignment	1
Alternate Route	11
Begin Again	21
Benefits	31
The Brown Bag	43
Chores	53
Chosen	65
Endure and Win!	75
Follow the GPS	85
He's Just that Into You	95

Launch	105
Legacy	115
Make Room for Jesus	125
Mentorship	135
New Place	145
Purposed Filled Life	155
Restoration	165
Seasons	175
Tug boat or Row boat?	185
You are a Miracle!	195

Introduction

The Everyday Miracles Instructor's Guide accompanies the Everyday Miracles Book and Everyday Miracles Music CD. The Everyday Miracles Instructor's Guide is simply that, a guide for small group study. The lessons in the Instructor's Guide can be adapted according to your group's needs. With the Instructor's Guide, your job of leading the group should be much easier. The pages that follow are suggestions for activities, discussions and other resources. For help, questions or comments, send an email to Julia@juliaroyston.com. I trust that your time together in small group study will be encouraging, enlightening and enjoyable. It's time to see the miracles that are happening every day!

Julia Royston

An Alignment

Are You Out of Alignment?

Teach me thy way, O Lord, and lead me in a plain path…" Psalms 27:11(KJV)

There are times we must take our car into the shop for a check-up because it is out of alignment. A car out of alignment pulls to one side of the road when the driver takes the hands off the wheel. The driver must hold the wheel steady so that the car will stay in the proper driving lane. Driving in an improper driving lane can cause an accident. Additionally, a car out of alignment can waste gas, put unnecessary wear on tires and cause extensive repair expense. Is your life out of alignment? Are your attitudes, spending habits or relationships out of alignment or balance? Are you on the verge of wasting resources, time and talent because of being out of alignment? Don't waste another day out of sync with the purpose God has for your life. Submit yourself to God for an alignment.

Align your mind with the mind of Christ
"…be ye transformed by the renewing of you mind…."   Romans 12:2 (KJV)

Align your heart by cleansing it with the word
"Now ye are clean through the word"…John 15:3 (KJV)

Align your spirit by receiving a fresh touch from the Holy Spirit
"He that believeth on me, the scripture hath said, out of his belly shall flow rivers of living water."   John 7:38 (KJV)

Align your feet by receiving orders from the Lord
"The steps of a good man are ordered by the lord and he delighteth in his way." Psalms 37:23 (KJV)

Prayer

Lord, hold us steady so that we can stay on the course that you have for our lives. Lord, we admit that we are out of alignment with Your way, will and word but we repent and return to you. Please forgive us Father. We begin again with you. We know that you are the chief mechanic and will tune us, turn us and tell us exactly what to do. We thank you for all these things. In Jesus' name, Amen.

Prayer Concerns

_____
_____
_____
_____
_____
_____
_____
_____
_____
_____
_____
_____
_____
_____
_____
_____
_____
_____

What do you need to do to get realigned?

Alignment

Journal/Reflect/Strategize

"Happiness is not a matter of intensity but of balance and order and rhythm and harmony."
Thomas Merton

"Next to love, balance is the most important thing." John Wooden

Devotional Objective: Align your life with God's word, His will and purpose for your life in multiple areas including but, not limited to ministry, work and family.

Materials Needed:
Everyday Miracles Book
Everyday Miracles Music CD
Holy Bible (version of your choice)
Worksheet Align1
Small scale
Small objects to be weighed
Checklist for routine oil change or tune-up - http://www.safetylca.org/s/safefact.asp?loc=s&tag=s3&pg=safe...&page=safefact_carmaintenance.htm – Preventative Vehicle Maintenance Checklist
http://www.aa-ownercenter.com/pdf/OC_WKST_maintenanceChecklist.pdf - Armour All Basic Maintenance Checklist
Dictionary of choice

Vocabulary:
Alignment
Balance
Accountability

Opening Activity: Open the meeting with Prayer. Ask for any announcements, celebrations or prayer concerns. Read the devotional and prayer on *Alignment*. (Note: this can be done silently, as a group or by one individual) Write down any prayer concerns. (Music can be played during the opening activity.) Ask the group for any comments or discussion on the scripture, devotional or prayer just read.

Questions to guide discussion: Ask yourself, is your life out of alignment or balance? Do you see some areas that need adjustments or realignment in your life? Do you spend more time working than time with family or alone time in meditation and rest? If your life is not realigned, where do you see yourself in the next 2-3 years? What are the first steps you need to take to begin the alignment process?

Activities

Activity #1 – Obtain a scale and give examples of how a scale should be balanced. Provide small items to be weighed or compared. If time permits, label the items to represent situations or problems that could get a life out of balance, e.g. work, too many obligations, wrong priorities, wrong friends.

Discussion: What could be done to bring the scale in balance? In turn, what are some things or areas that are out of balance in your life?

Response: Allow time for discussion and give examples of concrete ways to resolve these issues.

Activity #2 – Obtain a checklist for a car tune-up or oil change service from the websites listed.

Discussion: Ask the group if anyone has ever experienced any car problems that required a tune-up. How did these problems affect the performance of your car? Are there any problems in your life that are not allowing your life to run smooth? What are the solutions to these problems?

Response: Individuals can share with the group or journal their concerns later in the session.

Respond/Journal/Sharing

Respond: Each group member should receive a copy of Worksheet Align1. While the worksheets are being completed, play music from the Everyday Miracles Music CD.

Share: Allow group members the opportunity to gather in groups of 1-3 people for small group sharing. After 10 minutes or so, offer the opportunity for the whole group to share. (Note: If there are major alignment concern(s), pray for the person and their concern during this time or at the end as a closing prayer.)

Journal: Play a song from the Everyday Miracles Music CD and allow time for reflection/meditation and journaling. If time does not permit, journaling can be a home assignment.

Closing activity, thoughts and prayer

Closing activity: Allow the group time to exchange phone numbers or email addresses as an accountability partner to pray, encourage and empower them to continue making progress toward the goal of life alignment and balance.

Explain that an accountability partner in this instance does not require that you share every aspect of your personal affairs but, that the person is available for encouragement for spiritual growth.

Closing thoughts and prayer: God has great things in store for you if you obey and align yourself with His will, way and word. There are always consequences when you get out of alignment with God. Seek God daily and rely on His guidance and He will give you strength to make any adjustments in alignment. Pray that each group member will be strengthened, guided and assured that God has chosen and will equip them.

Follow-up Activities and/or Resources
- Read the next or assigned devotional prior to the next meeting time
- Listen to music provided on the music CDs
- Read Psalm 119
- At the next meeting, allow time for sharing a testimony regarding progress made as a follow-up to the Alignment lesson.
- Suggestion: Depending upon the duration of your group study sessions, there can always be an Alignment Lesson Part 2. Group Activity #2 can be used for the second week and the scripture Psalm 119 can be used as the scripture text for the Part 2 session.

Alignment

What is an area(s) that is/are out of balance or need to be aligned in your life?

_____
_____
_____
_____
_____
_____
_____
_____
_____
_____
_____
_____
_____
_____
_____
_____
_____
_____
_____
_____
_____
_____
_____

What steps need to be taken to bring your life in alignment?

Step 1:
_____
_____
_____
_____

Step 2:
_____
_____
_____
_____

Step 3:
_____
_____
_____
_____

Step 4:
_____
_____
_____
_____

Worksheet—Align1

Alternate Route

Which Way is Best?

"...let us run with patience the race that is set before us." Hebrews 12:1 (KJV)

Alternate Route

Recently in route to work, there was an accident and I exited the highway to take the local streets to arrive to work on time. The traffic required taking an alternate route. Time was spent going through stop lights, stop signs and slowing down for cars to turn off the main street to side streets and subdivisions. Seeing children playing or waiting for the bus, people walking their dogs and speaking to their neighbors was common place years ago. Traveling the streets instead of the highway is more time consuming. However, there is scenery travelling the local streets that can't be seen on the highway. New houses and businesses being built are seen while driving through the streets and not always seen from the highway. There are also people you meet on the street that you can't slow down to meet on the highway. Is your life taking an alternate route? Does it seem like others are travelling to their destiny on the German Autobahn super highway and you are on the streets going through the slow traffic and getting caught at every stoplight? Does it seem that you must always take the slower route to accomplish the plans of God for your life? There is a reason for everything. God knows where you need to be, as you are on life's journey. The alternate route you are taking is critical to the destiny God has planned for you. Don't worry about how others are travelling on their journey. You must run your race and complete it with integrity and the victory will be yours. Enjoy the miracle of the scenery and the people you meet while travelling the alternate route.

Prayer

God we thank you that you have great plans for us. Help us to be led by you to the specific places, people and positions that you have for us. Help us to not take for granted every detour that you have placed in our path. Help us to find the miracle that is in every experience. In Jesus' name I pray. Amen.

Prayer Concerns

_____
_____
_____
_____
_____
_____
_____
_____
_____
_____
_____
_____
_____
_____
_____
_____
_____
_____

Reflect on the many alternate routes in your life.

Alternate Route

Journal/Reflect/Strategize

Alternate Route

"The most important trip you may take in life is meeting people halfway." Henry Boye

For so was it charged me by the word of the LORD, saying, Eat no bread, nor drink water, nor turn again by the same way that thou camest. So he went another way, and returned not by the way that he came to Bethel. I Kings 13:9-10 (KJV)

Devotional Objective: Life is a journey with many twists, turns and different pathways to reach a destination. God's leading may take us in some unexpected places to have experiences that will enrich our lives.

Materials Needed
Everyday Miracles Book
Holy Bible (version of your choice)
Everyday Miracles Music CD
Physical road maps enough for groups of 2 or 3
As an alternative to physical road maps, access the Internet and point your browser to www.mapquest.com or www.maps.com
Regular Notebook Paper or Specialty paper enough for the group
Copies of Worksheet Altern1
Dictionary of choice

Vocabulary
Alternate
Route

Opening Activity Opening prayer. Allow time for celebrations, announcements or prayer concerns. Read the devotional and prayer titled, "Alternate Route" (Page 5 in the Everyday Miracles Book). Write down any current prayer concerns. (Music can be played during opening activity) Any comments or discussion on the scripture, devotional or prayer just read.

Questions to guide discussion: Have you ever taken an alternate route home and was pleasantly surprised at what you saw? What new things did you see? What new restaurants or businesses did you discover?

Activities:

Activity #1: Divide the group into groups of 2 or 3 people. Give each group a physical map. Each group should find the city where they reside on that map. Each group should locate a different city at least two states away. With the map markings only, map out a route to that city and complete Section 1 of Worksheet Altern1.

Activity #2: In this activity, the members will remain in the same group as activity #1 but, each group should find an alternate route to the same city they chose in activity #1. After finding an alternate route, complete Section 2 of Worksheet Altern1.

Respond/Share/Journal

Respond: Allow time for group to complete Worksheet Altern1.

Share: Each group will report on their destination city and what they discovered on their alternative routes. Each group should list at least one thing that they learned from the activity. After each group has shared, each individual should spend time journaling about the lesson, activity and/or their thoughts.

Journal: Play the song "Follow Me" on the Everyday Miracles Music CD and give group members an opportunity to write down a few thoughts about the Alternative Routes their lives have taken. What alternative routes has your life taken that you are now thankful but, at first, very hesitant? After a few minutes, allow time for a few group members to share their thoughts.

Closing activity, thoughts and prayer

Closing thoughts and prayer: Reiterate to the group that they should continue seeking and following God no matter how it looks. He is the conductor, director and cartographer or map maker of their lives. If you follow His map, you will arrive safely at your destination despite the mountains, rough terrain or narrow roads. Ask the group, will you be more or less willing to take an alternate route in the future? Pray for the leader, the entire group as well as one individual person for strength. Pray additionally for power and encouragement to continue with the study and a closer walk with Christ.

Follow-up Activity and/or Resources

- Read the next or assigned devotional prior to the next meeting time.
- Listen to music provided on the music CDs.
- Read Matthew 10:38; Matthew 16:24; John 12:26.
- At the next meeting, allow opportunity for sharing and /or testimony as a follow-up to the Alternate Routes lesson.

Alternate Route

Route #1

Current City:
_____

Destination City:
_____

List at least two cities along this route:

_____
_____

Are there any major attractions along this route? List at least 2 attractions:

_____
_____
_____
_____

Route #2

Same City as Route #1:
_____

Same Destination City as Route #1:
_____

List at least two different cities from route #1:

_____
_____

Are there any major attractions different from route #1? List at least 2 attractions:

_____
_____
_____
_____

Compare the two routes to the same city. Which is better? Why? What do you miss going in one direction compared to the other? Is one route more dangerous than the other or just different? Does one route take you through the small towns and avoid the highways and the other route is highway all of the way?

What have you learned?

Worksheet—Altern1

Begin Again

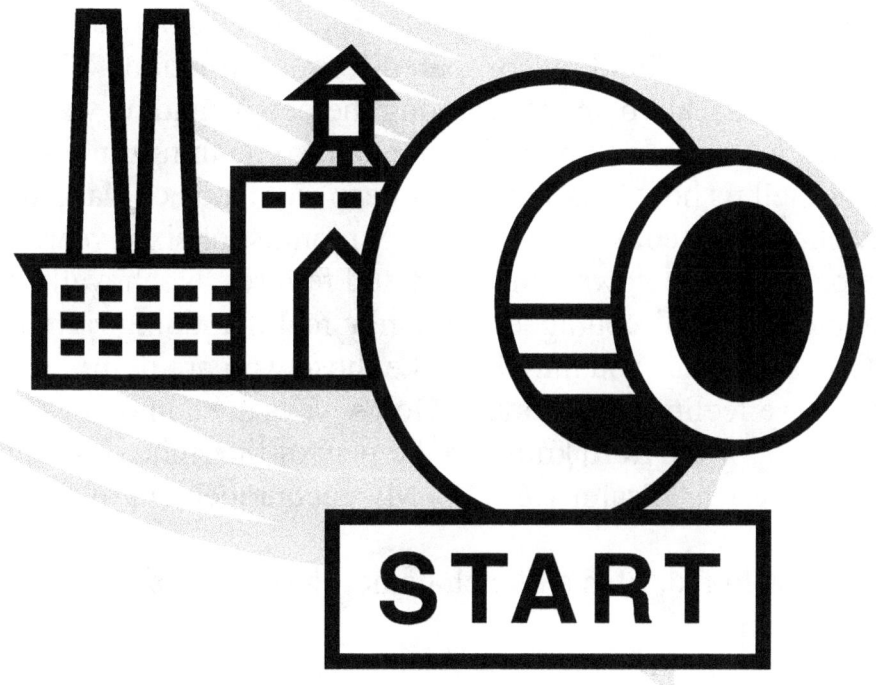

Where Do I Begin?

"Thus did Noah; according to all that God commanded him, so did he." Genesis 6:22 (KJV)

Begin Again

Genesis 6 refers to God's anger with the behavior of people on earth. The people were so wicked that their only thoughts were how to do more wickedness. Sound familiar? In Genesis 6:7, God decided to destroy most of the people and the animals from the earth and begin again. The destruction was by water, and God began again. Noah, and his family were spared from destruction. Why Noah? Because he was righteous and blameless among the people and he walked with God. (Genesis 6:9 NIV) God is looking to begin again some things in your life. The scripture did not tell us how long Noah had been righteous or walked with God. He could have been righteous six minutes, six months, or sixty years. Through the good, the bad, ups and downs, mistakes and failures, Noah walked with God. You may feel alone, and discouraged. You may feel that doing right is overlooked but, God sees you. You may feel like those who are doing wrong get ahead faster. These feelings are human. God's ways are sometimes slow but, God knows best. "For the Lord knoweth the way of the righteous: but the way of the ungodly shall perish." Psalm 1:6 KJV My encouragement to you is:

Stop. As with the old red, Etch a Sketch game, shake things up, wipe the slate clean and begin again.

Ask God. With a clean slate, no agenda, no plan, ask God. Begin asking God every day what he wants from your life in this season. Just because you have multiple gifts doesn't mean you are to use them all simultaneously.

Obey God. After you ask God, do it. God has the plan and knows specifically the method, strategy and the exact time of implementation. Beginning again may require you to be inactive so that you may plan, rest and regroup. You may think you have heard from God and you are moving in the right direction but, you may need to tweak some things or put some better systems in place.

Keep walking. Walking represents your life's journey. This life is not a sprint but, a marathon. This journey called life will require you to make some critical decisions. Don't be in a hurry to decide. Keep walking (living), listening and learning to wait for the answer.

Prayer

Thank you Father for loving me and wanting to use my gifts to bring glory to you. I surrender to your way and plan. In Jesus' name I pray. Amen.

Prayer Concerns

_____
_____
_____
_____
_____
_____
_____
_____
_____
_____
_____
_____
_____
_____
_____
_____

What current situation do you need to ask God to help you Begin Again?

Begin Again

Journal/Reflect/Strategize

Begin Again

"Beginnings are only difficult without any action." Byron Pulsifer

"Small opportunities are often the beginning of great enterprises." Demosthenes

But the pot he was shaping from the clay was marred in his hands; so the potter formed it into another pot, shaping it as seemed best to him. Jeremiah 18:4 (NIV)

Devotional Objective: There may have been some mistakes made in the past or opportunities that you missed but, you can begin again. God is a God of another chance and not just a second change. Take the time to ask Him for guidance and follow His specific directions and you can begin again.

Materials Needed
Everyday Miracles Book
Holy Bible (version of your choice)
Everyday Miracles Music CD
An etch-a-sketch (can be obtained from any toy store in miniature format)
Small puzzles (no more than 25 pieces to the puzzle)
Begin Again Worksheet – Begin1
Dictionary of choice

Vocabulary
Begin
Mistake
Fault
Sin

Opening Activity: Open with prayer. Allow time for celebrations, announcements and prayer concerns. Read the devotional and prayer titled, Begin Again (Page 9 of the Everyday Miracles Book) and write down any prayer concerns. (Music can be played during opening activity.) Open Discussion for any thoughts regarding the scripture or devotional.

Questions for Consideration: Have there been any projects that failed or opportunities in life that you missed? Why? What contributed to the incompletion of the task or success of the project? What should you have done differently or who should have you involved in the project for greater success?

Activities:

Activity #1 – Demonstrate the workings of an etch-a-sketch or distribute multiple etch-a-sketch toys to the group. Allow time to play for 2-3 minutes.

Discussion: Ask the group, what is fun and frustrating about an etch-a-sketch? Has any part of your life resembled an etch-a-sketch? Would you like to be able to erase parts of your life as easy as it is to erase an etch-a-sketch?

Activity #2 – With the small puzzles provided, divide the group into smaller groups of 2-4 people. Each group should put the puzzle pieces together without the benefit of seeing the finished picture of the puzzle. (Note: the puzzle pieces can be placed in another container or the top of the puzzle boxes removed) Give each group at least 10 minutes to attempt to put the puzzle together. Whether the puzzle is finished or not, disassemble the puzzle. Provide each group with the finished picture for each puzzle. Allow 5 minutes for the groups to put the puzzle pieces together a second time.

Discussion: What made the difference in your first attempt and the second? What did you learn from this activity?

Response /Share/Journal

Respond: Allow time for each person to complete Worksheet Begin1.

Share: If time allows, share thoughts about a project or task that they should Begin Again. What does beginning again mean to you?

Journal: Play the song "Begin Again" from the Everyday Miracles Music CD. Give time for journaling and writing a plan of action to Begin Again with a specific project. If someone has difficulty with things to journal about, feel free to ask the questions for consideration.

Closing activity, thoughts and prayer

Closing thoughts and Prayer: God has the finished picture for the etch-a-sketch and the puzzles. It is much easier to succeed at something when you have God as your guide to lead you to the finished product or destination. Seek God for guidance on a new project or endeavor. Begin Again with God. Pray that each group member will be strengthened, guided and assured that God has chosen and will equip them.

Follow-up Activity and/or Resources

- Read the next or assigned devotional prior to the next meeting time.
- Listen to music provided on the music CDs.
- Read Jeremiah 18.
- At the next meeting, allow opportunity for sharing and/or testimony as a follow-up on their progress of the Begin Again Lesson.

Begin Again

Write down at least 3 plans, goals or aspirations in your life that you wish you would begin again? Do you see why these goals never were reached or if reached, failed? Did you ever see an opportunity to begin again? Why or why not?

Goals	Success or Failure? Why?
1.	1.
2.	2.
3.	3.

Worksheet—Begin1

Benefits

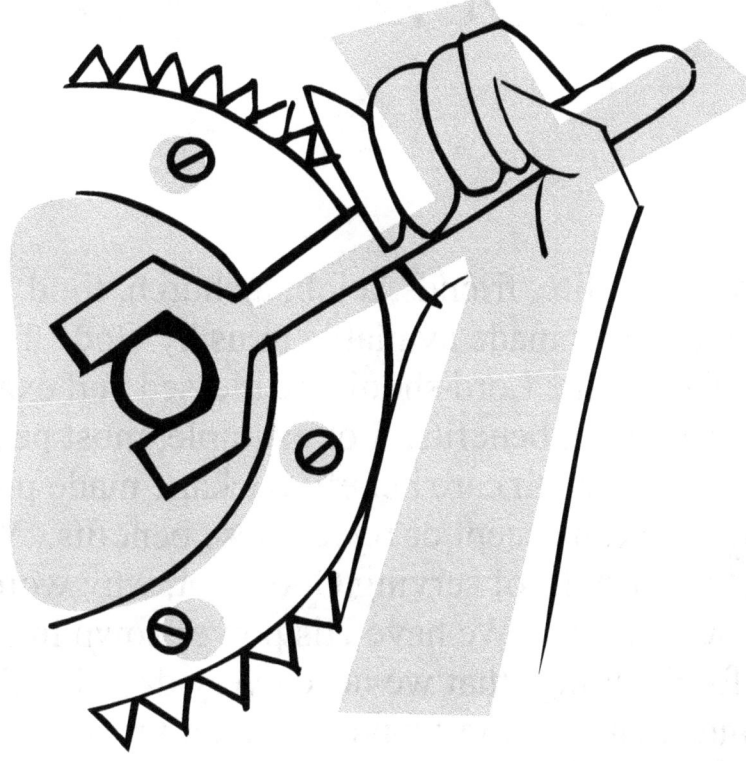

Count Your Benefits!

"Blessed be the Lord, who daily loadeth us with benefits, even the God of our salvation. Selah." Psalm 68:19 (KJV)

Benefits

Things such as breath, life, friends, a job, a church, food, clothes and shelter are daily benefits made available to us by God. The psalmist states in Psalm 68 that the Lord should be blessed and exalted because he provides us daily with benefits. For example, most people who work a full time job have a health care benefit package made possible by their employer. You can accept or reject these benefits. You can also accept or reject the benefit of serving God. But, why would you? We have His presence with us. We have His power down in us. We have His provision for the things that we need every day. Don't keep your eyes on the things that you don't have or haven't received. Most of these things are temporary and material. What non-material benefits do you now enjoy? Don't take things like health, love and family for granted. You will miss them when they are gone. During the recent hurricanes, cyclones, forest fires, we have seen the destruction and realize that no matter what we have we are really blessed. Are you looking for the miraculous? Do you have a new toy, gadget or luxury purchase on your mind? Before you buy it start counting the blessings that you already have received. It may be a surprise that you are already loaded down with many benefits and blessings beyond your wildest dreams.

Prayer

God we just thank you for all things. We thank you for the benefits of having a relationship with you. Please forgive us of being unthankful and wanting more things instead of more of you. In Jesus' name I pray. Amen

Prayer Concerns

_____
_____
_____
_____
_____
_____
_____
_____
_____
_____
_____
_____
_____
_____
_____
_____
_____

Count your benefits and not your deficits.

Journal/Reflect/Strategize

Benefits

"Our prayers should be for blessings in general, for God knows best what is good for us."
Socrates

"All the blessings we enjoy are Divine deposits, committed to our trust on this condition, that they should be dispensed for the benefit of our neighbors." John Calvin

What shall I render unto the LORD for all his benefits toward me? Psalm 116:12 (KJV)

Devotional Objective: The benefits of serving God out weigh any hardships, trials and tribulations in this present life and the life to come.

Materials Needed
Everyday Miracles Book
Holy Bible (version of your choice)
Everyday Miracles Music CD
Benefit Worksheet1
Benefit Worksheet 2
Dictionary of choice

Vocabulary
Benefit
Tribulation
Trial
Hardship

Opening Activity: Open with prayer. Allow time for celebrations, announcements and prayer concerns. Read the devotional and prayer entitled, Benefits (Page 15 and write a list of prayer concerns. (Music can be played during opening activity.) Allow time to share thoughts regarding the scripture or devotional.

    Questions to guide discussion: How do you feel about the many benefits that you have been given? What should be your response to God for all of the many benefits that you have received?

Activities
    Activity #1: Each group member should receive a copy of Benefit Worksheet1 and Benefit Worksheet2.

Discussion: As a group, vocalize the benefits that a person could receive on his job. Each person should list these benefits on their own Benefit Worksheet 1. After the list is compiled, ask each person to circle the benefits that they do not have on their job. (Note: Ask the group members not to vocalize what benefits they don't receive on their particular job. This is an individual exercise to be used to make a point later in the lesson)

Activity #2: For this activity, each group member will complete Benefit Worksheet 2.

Discussion: As a group, vocalize the benefits of a relationship with God through Jesus Christ. Each group member should write a list of the benefits as they are given. (Note: Point out to the entire group that they all have access to these benefits if they are in relationship with Jesus Christ.)

Respond/Share/Journal

Respond: What does the word "benefits" mean to you now as opposed to before this lesson?

Share: Allow group members to share their thoughts. (Note: As the facilitator, formulate your own questions based on the responses from the group members to continue discussion)

Journal: Play a song from the Everyday Miracles Music CD. Give time for journaling and writing a plan of action as to how they are allowing the Benefits of God to benefit others. If someone has difficulty with things to journal about, feel free to ask the questions for consideration. (Suggestion: the journaling exercise can be an entry thanking God for all of His benefits.)

Closing activity, thoughts and prayer

Closing thoughts and Prayer: The benefit of having a relationship with Jesus Christ is the same for everyone who accepts Him as Lord and Savior. Some people don't enjoy all of the benefits but, it doesn't mean that they don't have access to these benefits. If you distributed the Benefit Worksheet 1 papers, you will notice that each of the benefit packages of each company will be different. Some companies provide more benefits than others. Unlike company benefits, we have access to all of the promises/benefits listed in the Bible. What a blessing! Pray for strength, power and encouragement that all will continue to study and develop a closer walk with Christ.

Extension Activity: Is there anyone in the group who needs a job or a job with benefits? Is there a member of the group who can provide job leads for the unemployed group member? Pray for employment guidance for the unemployed group member and the unemployed throughout the world.

Follow-up Activity and/or Resources
- Read the next or assigned devotional prior to the next meeting time.
- Listen to music provided on the Everyday Miracles music CDs.
- Read Psalm 68
- At the next meeting, allow opportunity for sharing and/ or testimony as a follow-up on their progress of the Benefits Lesson.

Benefits

If you work a full-time, part-time or job share, what are some of the benefits that you have available to you on your job? Are there any benefits that you have access to that you don't take advantage of? Why or why not?

_____
_____
_____
_____
_____
_____
_____
_____
_____
_____
_____
_____
_____
_____
_____
_____
_____
_____
_____
_____
_____
_____
_____
_____
_____
_____
_____
_____

Worksheet—Benefit1

Benefits

List the benefits of being in relationship to God through Jesus Christ. Do all of your benefits fit on this sheet? What do I give to God in exchange for all of the benefits He gives to me?

_____
_____
_____
_____
_____
_____
_____
_____
_____
_____
_____
_____
_____
_____
_____
_____
_____
_____
_____
_____
_____
_____
_____
_____
_____
_____
_____
_____
_____
_____
_____
_____
_____
_____
_____

Worksheet—Benefit2

Brown Bag

The Brown Bag of Expectation

"My soul, wait thou only upon God; for my expectation is from him."
Psalm 62:5 (KJV)

The Brown Bag

Whenever my grandmother went to a funeral she would bring along a brown paper bag. Just in case she went to the cemetery she would be ready. Ready for what you ask? To pick some wild dandelion green vegetables if found in the cemetery growing on their own. If my grandmother found some greens, she didn't ask anybody, she bent over and started picking the greens and putting them in her bag. Those greens in the cemetery were passed by, overlooked and walked on by others but, my grandmother didn't miss them. Do you have your brown bag of expectation prepared for what God could bring in your life? Are you making room in your mind, soul and heart to receive what you've been praying for? I don't know whether my grandmother daily prayed for greens to be in the cemetery but, she was prepared with her bag, kept her eyes peeled and combing the ground just in case. Have you got your brown paper bag ready? Are your eyes opened and is your heart receptive to not pass by what others deem unimportant but, could be a great blessing to you and your household? In the hands of my grandmother, some greens from the cemetery could be a great side to a meal. What has God spoken to you by His word or placed in your heart that you are still waiting to receive? Don't miss the opportunity. Get yourself prepared. Go get your brown bag.

Prayer

God I thank you that you have placed the brown bag of expectation in my life. Help me to be observant and open to the things that you have for my life. I thank you in advance. In Jesus' Name I pray. Amen

Prayer Concerns

_____
_____
_____
_____
_____
_____
_____
_____
_____
_____
_____
_____
_____
_____
_____
_____

What are you waiting to receive from the Lord? Do you have your brown bag ready?

The Brown Bag

Journal/Reflect/Strategize

The Brown Bag

"All the great spiritual leaders in history were people of hope. Abraham, Moses, Ruth, Mary, Jesus, Rumi, Gandhi, and Dorothy Day all lived with a promise in their hearts that guided them toward the future without the need to know exactly what it would look like. Let's live with hope."
Henri J. Nouwen

For I know that this shall turn to my salvation through your prayer, and the supply of the Spirit of Jesus Christ, According to my earnest expectation and my hope, that in nothing I shall be ashamed, but that with all boldness, as always, so now also Christ shall be magnified in my body, whether it be by life, or by death. For to me to live is Christ, and to die is gain. Philippians 1:19-21

Devotional Objective: Our confidence, expectations and hope should remain all in Christ. Although we have earthly expectations and desires, we should make sure that they are fueled with pure motives. If we pray and expect God to fulfill His promises to us, we should prepare for the manifestation. As much as we expect from God, He is expecting certain things from us.

Materials Needed
Everyday Miracles Book
Holy Bible (version of your choice)
Everyday Miracles Music CD
Brown bags for each group member
Small gift for each group member (Note: the gift can be pieces of candy, if the group is rather large, or a small inexpensive gift for each group member)
Brown Worksheet 1
Dictionary of choice

Vocabulary
Expectation
Hope
Manifest

Opening Activity Open with prayer. Allow time for celebrations, announcements and prayer concerns. Read the devotional and prayer entitled, Brown Bag (Page 19 in the Everyday Miracles Book) and write down any prayer concerns. (Music can be played during opening activity.) Allow time for thoughts regarding the scripture or devotional.

Questions for Consideration: What are some expectations you have of God? Why do you think that He hasn't done them yet or possibly said, no? What are some realistic expectations you have for your life? Why do you think you don't have some of these things in your life yet? What should you be doing to prepare yourself for these new things to come about in your life?

Activities:

Activity #1 – Each group member should receive a brown bag. With a pencil, each member is write on the brown bag some prayer requests or expectations that they have from the Lord.
Discussion: After each group member has completed writing on the bag, ask them, are these realistic expectations or fantasies? Will these expectations harm anyone else or just benefit you? In other words, are these God expectations or just selfish wants? Allow time for group member discussion. What did you learn? Do any of these expectations need to be removed from the list?

Activity #2 – Notify the group that they are each going to receive an unexpected gift to be placed in their brown bag.
Discussion: After they receive the gift, ask them how it felt to receive something unexpected?

Activity #3 – Each group member should turn the brown bag over to the blank side.
Discussion: On this side of the brown bag, ask the group members to write expectations they have for themselves. What do you believe God expects from you? What is your part to play in receiving what you expect from God? What do you expect from yourself? Do you have high or low expectations of yourself? Allow time for discussion after minutes of recording the group member's thoughts.

Respond/Share/Journal

Respond: – After reviewing your expectation list you wrote down on the brown bag, do some of the things that you are expecting now seem unimportant? What are you going to do about the things/projects/issues God expects you to take care of?
Share: Allow time for individuals to share with the group.
Journal: Play the song "When You Pray" from the Everyday Miracles Music CD. Give time for journaling and writing a plan of action on Worksheet Brown1 in response to the Brown Bag lessons. Journal about a specific project or need for guidance from God regarding a desire or expectation. (Note: If someone has difficulty with things to journal about, feel free to ask the questions for consideration.)

Closing activity, thoughts and prayer

Closing thoughts and Prayer: The grandmother in the devotional went to the cemetery with a brown bag. She knew there was a possibility that wild greens could be growing in the cemetery. She had picked wild greens in a cemetery before. Are you going to the wrong places expecting something that isn't going to be there or has no possibility of being found in that particular place? Make sure that your expectations are God centered and not covetous or selfish in their motives. Pray for strength, power and encouragement that all will continue to study and develop a closer walk with Christ.

Extension Activity: Write an action plan. What do you need to do to prepare for your expectation? What are the steps that need to be taken to make this expectation a reality? Set a timeline to complete the plan of action.

Follow-up Activity and/or Resources
- Read the next or assigned devotional prior to the next meeting time.
- Listen to music provided on the Everyday Miracles music CDs.
- Read Jeremiah 17:13, Psalm 25:3, Hebrews 11:1.
- At the next meeting, allow opportunity for sharing and or testimony as a follow-up on their progress of the Brown Bag Lesson.

Brown Bag

Are you expecting anything from the Lord? List it here...

What do you believe the Lord is expecting from you?

What do you need to do to prepare for the things God has for you?

Worksheet—Brown1

Chores

So Many Chores, So Little Time.

"Thou preparest a table before me in the presence of mine enemies: thou anointest my head with oil; my cup runneth over." Psalm 23:5 (KJV)

Chores

Have you ever wished there were a dish fairy that would come to your house and wash dishes every night? Sure there are people that can afford housekeepers or cleaning services but, the average household must keep their own house clean. The repetition of washing dishes, clothes and floors seems tedious at times to say the least but, essential for keeping a clean house. In spite of our complaints of these chores, our ancestors would surely scold us because we have the convenience of mechanical dishwashers. They had to wash dishes in creeks, tubs or other make shift sinks after carrying water in from outside wells or streams. Think about what would happen if you had no food to eat, clothes to wear or a place to keep clean? You would be hungry, naked and homeless. But, the dirty dishes proves that God provided food one more time. The dirty clothes to be washed prove that God provided for us and we are not naked. The dirty house to be cleaned proves that God provided you a house, whether you rent or own, to get dirty enough to have to clean. Thank you Lord for having chores. David declared in Psalm 23 that God would prepare a table before him in the presence of his enemies and his cup would run over. Paul said that God would supply all of our need according to His riches in glory Philippians 4:19. Thank God for His promises of provision for our households. Praise the Lord for chores!

Prayer

God, we thank you for your provision. Help us to see and be grateful daily for this provision. Jehovah Jireh you are our provider. In Jesus' Name we pray. Amen.

Prayer Concerns

_____
_____
_____
_____
_____
_____
_____
_____
_____
_____
_____
_____
_____
_____
_____
_____

Thank God for your chores.

Chores

I see dishes just more dishes
It leaves me wishing for more than dishes
I see laundry just more laundry
I in a quandary for more than just laundry

Have you ever been hungry for more?
The longing for more than the daily chore
It made you want to leave right out of the front door
But you keep coming back for the ones that you adore

Where is the passion, fire and light?
Where is the thrill of waking to another daylight?
It's buried under the drudgery of duty
Not lit by purpose to a pathway of destiny

The necessary must be done
Imagine a house with dishes, laundry and cleaning left undone
It's a sin, crime and shame
The cleaning police must come

But, what about the human house inside?
The interior dreams unrealized
The lawn of ideas unfertilized
The benefits of education un-materialized

The dishes of duty now in the sink
The dust of determination failing and on the brink
The carpet of continuation threatens to rip
The bathroom of boredom like a faucet's annoying drip

Stop the depression, gloom and sadness
Stop the moaning, whining and madness
Look in the mirror you're still here and alive
Start looking at what's right and the light will arise

You may be tired and weary
But, you're still breathing though the way may be dreary
Stop, look at your circumstance, really
Refocus your eyes, I'm calling, just hear me

The dirty dish proved that there was food on the plate
God, Jehovah Jireh provided on time and not late
The dirty laundry proved that there are still clothes are your back
God, the Almighty won't leave you naked or in lack

The dirty house that needs to be clean
Means that you have a house and not just a bridge or shelter on which to lean
That carpet that needs a few passes of a vacuum
Could have been the grass covering your tomb

Praise God for the chores to be done
Praise God for what you have and know that there is more to come
Praise God and let the dishes, laundry and vacuum sing
Praise God for Everything!

Journal/Reflect/Strategize

Chores

"Act as if what you do makes a difference. It does." William James

"We can do no great things, only small things with great love." Mother Teresa

*But my God shall supply all your need according to his riches in glory by Christ Jesus.
Philippians 4:19 (KJV)*

...and the LORD blessed Obededom, and all his household. 2 Samuel 6:11 (KJV)

Devotional Objective: Daily and weekly chores in a household are often tedious, time consuming and tiring but, with each chore, see God's provision working in your daily life.

Materials Needed
Everyday Miracles Book
Holy Bible (version of your choice)
Everyday Miracles Music CD
Worksheet Chore1
Provide examples of cleaning supplies. For example, rubber gloves, dishwashing detergent, dust pan, etc.
Dictionary of choice

Vocabulary
Chore
Provision

Opening Activity: Open with prayer. Allow time for celebrations, announcements and prayer concerns. Read the devotional, prayer and poem entitled, Chores (Page 23 from the Everyday Miracles Book) and write any prayer concerns. (Music can be played during opening activity.) Share any thoughts regarding the scripture, devotional or poem.

Questions for Consideration: Are there chores and routine household duties you hate doing each day or week? What would happen if these chores went undone? What if you were homeless and had no place to do these chores? Do you now feel differently about doing chores?

Activities:

Activity #1 – Hold up the cleaning supplies that you have provided.

Discussion: Rehearse what you use the cleaning supplies to clean and why? What would happen if you didn't clean these areas in your home? Why do you dread cleaning?

Activity #2 – Each group member will complete Worksheet Chore1 individually.

Discussion: The entire group will divide into groups of 2-3. If there is a smaller study group, allow individuals to share with the entire group.

Respond/Share/Journal

Respond: After you have reviewed the list of chores and discussed the person that does the chore, is there a blessing in the chores you listed?

Share: Allow individuals to share with their responses to the entire group.

Journal: Play a song from the Everyday Miracles Music CD and give time for journaling about the chores, provision and blessings in your household. (Note: If someone has difficulty with things to journal about, feel free to ask the questions for consideration.)

Closing activity, thoughts and prayer

Closing Thoughts and Prayer: Remind the group members that there is a blessing in each chore because it demonstrates the provision of God in your household. The dirty clothes show that God has provided clothing. Another day at work, demonstrates that there is employment and a means of providing income for your house. Praise and thank God for the many chores that represent the provision in your entire household. Pray for strength, power and encouragement that all will continue to study and develop a closer walk with Christ

Extension Activity: If there is a need among the group members, allow time for the expression of that need. Pray for provision and/or someone in the group to be the supplier of that need.

Follow-up Activity and Resources
- Read the next or assigned devotional prior to the next meeting time.
- Listen to music provided on the Everyday Miracles music CDs.
- Read the entire book of Ruth.
- At the next meeting, allow opportunity for sharing and or testimony as a follow-up on their progress of the Chores Lesson.

Chores

List the chores that you have to do daily and weekly in your house. What would happen if these chores didn't get done? What could possibly be the blessing of each chore?

Worksheet—Chore 1

Chosen

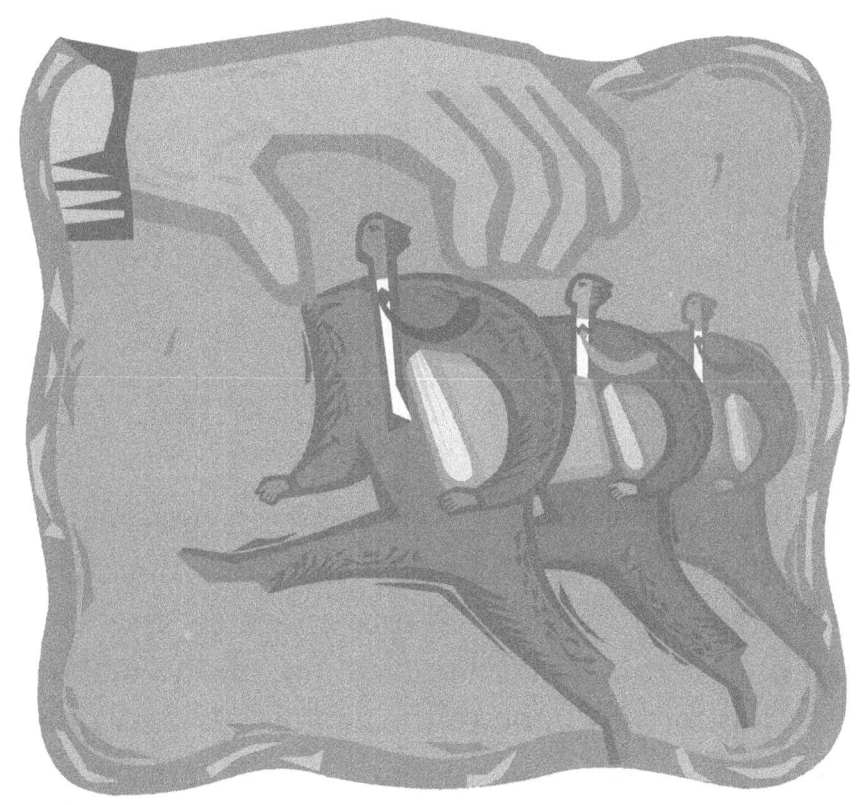

You Are Chosen

"Ye have not chosen me, but I have chosen you…" John 15:16 (KJV)

"But ye are a chosen generation, a royal priesthood, an holy nation, a peculiar people; that ye should shew forth the praises of him who hath called you out of darkness into his marvellous light..: I Peter 2:9 (KJV)

Chosen

In elementary school, my heart would cringe each recess or gym class when team sports were to be played. I was not athletic at all. The captains were selected and then they in turn chose the most athletic students as team members. Oh the humiliation, oh the embarrassment of standing there waiting until one of the captains would finally say, "okay, I'll take Julia". On the other hand, if there were a musical part, I was always chosen first. Each of us has been given a gift, talent or job that they do well. It is always an honor to be chosen. In any area of life, whether its dating, academics, community committees or employment, people like to be chosen. It makes them feel special and important. To be chosen means, you would be an asset to that team. God is making a choice and He chooses you. God values you. God gave his son Jesus to prove his love and commitment to you. God has settled on a permanent love and yes, it's you. No matter your level of ability, looks or talent, God chooses you.

Prayer

Father we thank you that you have chosen us when we wouldn't choose ourselves. We thank you that you love us unconditionally and without reservation. Help us to choose you, your plan and your way every day. In Jesus Name I pray. Amen.

Prayer Concerns

_____
_____
_____
_____
_____
_____
_____
_____
_____
_____
_____
_____
_____
_____
_____
_____

Why do you think God chose you? If not sure, thank God and then ask Him for the reason why you are chosen.

Chosen

Journal/Reflect/Strategize

"I don't know what your destiny will be, but one thing I do know: the only ones among you who will be really happy are those who have sought and found how to serve." Albert Schweitzer

For thou art an holy people unto the LORD thy God, and the LORD hath chosen thee to be a peculiar people unto himself, above all the nations that are upon the earth.
Deuteronomy 14:2 (NIV)

Devotional Objective: We are all chosen by God for a purpose, a reason and with a specific gift or talent. Delight in the fact that no matter who doesn't select you, Jesus said, "I have chosen you". Jesus has chosen you for His team to fulfill His purpose in the earth through you.

Materials Needed
Everyday Miracles Book
Holy Bible (version of your choice)
Everyday Miracles Music CD
Small toys/gifts – one opened and another one still in the original package.
(Note: provide at least 3 examples)
Worksheet Chosen1
Worksheet Chosen2
Dictionary of choice

Vocabulary
Chosen
Gift
Selected

Opening Activity: Open with prayer. Allow time for celebrations, announcements and prayer concerns. Read the devotional and prayer entitled, Chosen (Page 29 from the Everyday Miracles Book) and write any prayer concerns. (Music can be played during opening activity.) Share any thoughts regarding the scripture, devotional or prayer.

Questions for Consideration: What do you think that God has chosen you to do? If you are not sure, what do you enjoy doing? Why do you think that God chose you? Would you have chosen yourself? How does it make you feel when you are chosen for an assignment or project?

Activities:

Activity #1: To demonstrate an example of choice or choosing show the group two identical toys. One toy that is dirty and the other toy that is new. Also show a toy with the package opened and the other toy still in the package.

Discussion: Which toy did they choose? Second example of choosing could be, provide two brown paper bags with a small prize or something inside. On the outside of the bag or on a separate card, provide a description of the contents of the bag. The one description should be very attractive to the group and the other description can be very vague. Which bag would they choose and why?

Activity #2: On the Worksheet Chosen1, list the gifts or talents that you possess. On the Worksheet Chosen2, ask someone else in the group to list at least 2 gifts or talents that you possess.

Discussion: Compare Worksheet Chosen1 that you completed with the Worksheet Chosen2 that your neighbor completed. Are they similar? Does your neighbor see something in you that you don't see in yourself or vice versa?

Response/Share/Journal

Respond: What did you learn about being chosen? What did you learn about your own motives and reasons for choosing one thing over the other? After this lesson, will you choose differently? Why or why not?

Share: Allow individuals to share with their responses to the entire group.

Journal: Play a song from the Everyday Miracles Music CD and give time for journaling about being Chosen. (Note: If someone has difficulty with things to journal about, feel free to ask the questions for consideration.)

Closing activity, thoughts and prayer

Closing Thoughts and Prayer: Remind the group members that they are chosen by God to fulfill His purpose on the earth. God will give them the knowledge, power and endurance to complete any task. They are chosen and will be equipped to do the job, complete the project and savor the victory. For the closing prayer, divide the group into pairs. Pray that each group member will be strengthened, guided and assured that God has chosen and will equip them.

Follow-up Activity and Resources

- Read the next or assigned devotional prior to the next meeting time.
- Listen to music provided on the Everyday Miracles music CDs.
- Read the entire book of Esther.
- At the next meeting, allow opportunity for sharing and/or testimony as a follow-up on their progress of the Chosen Lesson.

Chosen

List the gifts and talents God has placed inside of you. Are you using them for His glory?

_____
_____
_____
_____
_____
_____
_____
_____
_____
_____
_____
_____
_____
_____
_____
_____
_____
_____
_____
_____
_____
_____
_____
_____
_____
_____
_____
_____
_____
_____

Worksheet—Chosen 1

Exchange this sheet with another group member. List the gifts and talents that others see in you. Are you using them for His glory?

Worksheet—Chosen2

Endure and Win

Endurance = Victory

"Thou therefore endure hardness, as a good soldier of Jesus Christ..No man that warreth entangleth himself with the affairs of this life; that he may please him who hath chosen him to be a soldier. The husbandman that laboureth must be first partaker of the fruits." 2 Timothy 2:3-4, 6(KJV)

Endure and Win!

Have you ever run a race or taken a long walk? You start out running or walking full of energy and positive attitude. After several minutes, you begin to get tired, breathing heavy and you want to stop. You can't stop because you have already walked too far. You don't want to turn around and have to walk or run back. You can't stop you must keep moving forward. Whether you turn back or complete the entire course, you have to keep moving. No matter how hard it is or tired you feel, you must endure. The object is to build stamina, endurance and eventually be victorious. In the second letter to Timothy, the Apostle Paul gives Timothy three examples of individuals that work hard carrying out difficult assignments or tasks. Soldiers, athletes and farmers all have assignments that require hard work and discipline. Paul admonishes and encourages Timothy to endure hardness as a good soldier, run a great race like a good athlete and work hard like a good farmer. No matter what comes your way you must continue, keep at it and finish. Endure the hard times so you can receive the medal-of-honor like a soldier, win at the finish line as an athlete or receive a great harvest like the farmer. If you continue, you will endure and eventually win.

Prayer

Lord, I thank you that you suffered for me to give me the free gift of eternal life. I ask that you give me strength to endure each day. With your power inside, I know that I can complete the task and receive the prize. In Jesus' Name I pray. Amen.

Prayer Concerns

_____
_____
_____
_____
_____
_____
_____
_____
_____
_____
_____
_____
_____
_____
_____
_____
_____

Encourage yourself to endure and win.

Endure and Win!

Journal/Reflect/Strategize

Endure and Win

"There is one quality that one must possess to win, and that is definiteness of purpose, the knowledge of what one wants, and a burning desire to possess it." Napoleon Hill

"Accept challenges, so that you may feel the exhilaration of victory." George S. Patton

I have fought a good fight, I have finished my course, I have kept the faith...
2 Timothy 4:7 (KJV)

Devotional Objective: This life is a journey and an endurance test not a short jog or sprint. If you are to obtain the prize of living the abundant life, you must realize that it is a process of endurance. The one who does not quit is the one who will win the race and get the gold medal.

Materials Needed
Every Miracles Book
Holy Bible (version of your choice)
Everyday Miracles Music CD
Internet access and visit www.olympics.org – The official Olympics website.
Guest Speaker from outside or within the group who specializes in physical endurance training or other physical activity training.
Worksheet Endure1
Dictionary of your choice

Suggestion for this session: A personal trainer or someone who is active in physical fitness could come and speak to the group concerning endurance training or exercise. What are the keys to endurance training? How do you prepare yourself physically, mentally and emotionally for physical activity? Who are the people that influenced your training endeavors? What keeps you motivated to continue?

Vocabulary
Endurance
Victory
Journey

Opening Activity: Open with prayer. Allow time for celebrations, announcements and prayer concerns. Read the devotional and prayer entitled, "Endure and Win", (Page 33 of the Everyday Miracles Book) and write down any prayer concerns. (Music can be played during opening activity.) Share any thoughts regarding the scripture, devotional or prayer.

Questions to guide discussion: Is there a situation, problem or person that you've been dealing with for a long time? Do you want to quit? Can you remember another situation that you endured and won? How did that feel once it was over? Was it worth it? With that past experience, what did it teach you about enduring? How can your endurance test help someone else?

Activities:
Activity #1: Show the entire group an excerpt from an exercise video.
Discussion: After seeing the video, how did it make you feel? Why do you think that they are able to endure? Do you think that you could do the exercises on the video? Why or why not?

Respond/Share/Journal
Respond: Each group member should have a copy of Worksheet Endure1 and complete the survey about their endurance level. The endurance survey not only refers to physical endurance but, also social and emotional endurance.
Share: After completing the worksheet alone, the group members should turn to a partner and share their responses.
Journal: Play a song from the Everyday Miracles Music CD and give time for journaling about Endurance and Winning. (Note: If someone has difficulty with things to journal about, feel free to ask the questions for consideration.)

Closing activity, thoughts and prayer
Closing Thoughts and Prayer: Remind the group that winners never quit and quitters never win. This spiritual race is a journey but, you will only make it with God's help. Even when others walk away and/or tell you to quit, ask God for help and keep going. Endurance = Victory. Pray that each group member will be strengthened, guided and assured that God has chosen and will equip them.

Extension Activity: Issue a challenge to the group. If you are not physically active, try walking 1 block a day. The next week you should walk 2 blocks a day. Increase your physical activity daily until you are walking at least a 1 mile a day.

Follow-up Activity and Resources
- Read the next or assigned devotional prior to the next meeting time.
- Listen to music provided on the Everyday Miracles music CDs.
- Read Psalm 118.
- At the next meeting, allow opportunity for sharing and or testimony as a follow-up on their progress of the "Endure and Win" Lesson.

Endure and Win

Activity	Endurance Level			
Walking up and down stairs	No	Low	Medium	High
Walking 1 mile	No	Low	Medium	High
Walking 2 miles	No	Low	Medium	High
Marathon	No	Low	Medium	High
People who criticize me.	No	Low	Medium	High
People who talk behind my back	No	Low	Medium	High
People who confront me about an issue	No	Low	Medium	High
Cruel Boss or Supervisor	No	Low	Medium	High
Uncommitted church committee member	No	Low	Medium	High
Unfaithful leadership	No	Low	Medium	High

****
Turn to a partner and discuss your answers. What were your results?

Worksheet—Endure1

God's Plan Successful

Follow God's GPS

"Howbeit when he, the Spirit of truth, is come, he will guide you into all truth...."
John 13:16 (KJV)

Follow the GPS

(God's Plan Successful)

On a recent bus trip, there was a GPS or Global Positioning System on the dash board. In spite of the GPS, we took several wrong turns and arrived at several destinations late. We visited states that were not on the trip's itinerary and wasted much gas and time. The driver did not follow the directions of the GPS. The voice on the GPS system was loud and clear, yet we got lost. Have you felt led to go in a specific direction and ignored it? Have you ever realized later that you missed a great opportunity because you didn't listen and obey? If you are a Christian, that is the leading of the Holy Spirit. The Spirit is there to lead and guide into all truth. The Holy Spirit is your heavenly GPS. Do we ask for guidance of the Holy Spirit GPS system? Do we follow the instructions? Have you ever found yourself going in circles? You seem to have passed this same gas station, church or people two or three times without reaching your destination. I have seen the results of not following the earthly and heavenly GPS System. It can be life altering and can take months or years to get back on track. Don't get distracted and miss your turn. You must listen and follow the GPS!

Prayer

Lord we thank you for the Holy Spirit down inside of us. We ask that you forgive us for not following your directions and going our own way. We are sorry. Help us now to follow you and trust that you have a great plan and future for us. In Jesus' Name I pray. Amen.

Prayer Concerns

_____
_____
_____
_____
_____
_____
_____
_____
_____
_____
_____
_____
_____
_____
_____
_____

While following the Holy Spirit, I…..

Follow the GPS

Journal/Reflect/Strategize

God's Plan Successful

"Planning is bringing the future into the present so that you can do something about it now."
Alan Lakein

Devotional Objective: If we are to fulfill God's divine plan for our lives, we must follow His directions, His leading and His plan.

Materials Needed
Everyday Miracles Book
Holy Bible (version of your choice)
Everyday Miracles Music CD
Napkins for each member of the group
Worksheet GPS1
Dictionary of your choice

Vocabulary
Directions
Plan
Guidance

Opening Activity: Open with prayer. Allow time for celebrations, announcements and prayer concerns. Read the devotional and prayer entitled, God's Plan Successful, (Page 37 from the Everyday Miracles Book) and jot down any prayer concerns. (Music can be played during opening activity.) Share any thoughts regarding the scripture, devotional or prayer.

Questions to guide discussion: Has there been a time that you heard God's voice and you didn't follow? Was there a time that you read a command in God's word that you didn't follow? Why or why not? What was the result of the disobedience? Did the results last long-term or short-term? What caused the hesitation in obeying God?

Activities:
Activity #1 – Similar to the childhood "Simon says" game, ask everyone to stand. If there is room, the group can form a circle and move slightly from their seats to give them room. The facilitator should repeat several instructions for the group, i.e. take one step forward, take one step backward, lift your right hand, lift your left hand, etc.

Discussion: Are there some group members who follow verbal directions better than others? How did you feel about following the simple directions? What if the directions had been something more difficult?

Response: Allow time for discussion about following verbal or spoken directions.

Activity #2 – Each group member should receive a napkin and the Worksheet GPS1. Each group member should then follow the directions on the Worksheet GPS1 with the napkin they have been given. If there is a problem with an individual completing either activity, show them or model the activity.

Discussion: Did the napkin turn out like the picture? Why or why not?

Respond/Share/Journal

Respond: Remind the group to think about both activities. Which directions are easier to follow, the verbal in group activity #1 or written directions group activity#2? Once someone showed you how to complete the activity, was this easier or more difficult?

Share: Allow time for discussion.

Journal: Play the song "Follow Me" on the Everyday Miracles Music CD and give time for journaling about God's Plan Successful. (Note: If someone has difficulty with things to journal about, feel free to ask the questions for consideration.)

Closing activity, thoughts and prayer

Closing Thoughts and Prayer: God has the plan for your life. God will give you direction on what you need to do to fulfill His plan for your life. He may speak to you through a song, in an audible voice, through His word, through a preacher, teacher or friend. He will get the directions to you. The most important thing is for you to follow His directions. God wants you to succeed. He died to prove how much He loves you and wants what's best for you. Are you willing to follow His directions? Pray that each group member will be strengthened, guided and assured that God has chosen and will equip them.

Extension Activity: In the next week, if you have a GPS system, obtain the address of somewhere you have never visited. Put the address in your GPS system and follow the directions. Report your findings at the next group meeting.

Follow-up Activity and Resources

- Read the next or assigned devotional prior to the next meeting time.
- Listen to music provided on the Everyday Miracles music CD.
- Read the Book of Jonah.
- At the next meeting, allow opportunity for sharing and or testimony as a follow-up

God's Plan Successful

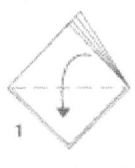
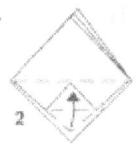
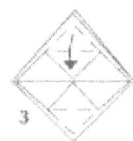
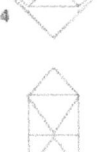

Diamond Paper Fold

1. Place the napkin in a diamond shape, with the open corner points up and fold the first layer of the top point down to meet the bottom point.
2. Fold that same point to meet the center line.
3. Fold the second point from the top to meet the center line
4. Fold the side points back and away from you so that they overlap in the back.

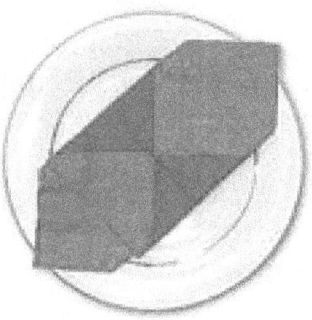

Does your napkin look like the picture? What went wrong? Did you not understand the directions? Would it have been easier if someone had shown you first then you do it after the demonstration?

Worksheet—GPS1

He's Just that Into You!

Are you into Him?

Casting all your care upon him; for he careth for you. " I Peter 5:7 (KJV)

He's Just that into You!

In 2004, Greg Behrendt released the book "He's just not that into you". This book is a relationship/dating book from the male perspective. This author was willing to offer women a reason why some men would not commit to marriage or even a long term relationship. The conclusion was, "He's just not that into you". Have you ever invested time and money into a person and suddenly realize that it was not going to work out? You were optimistic, hopeful and working hard to make the relationship work only to find out that you were in it alone. It does take two to tango. Well, there is a Person that is very much into you. He is concerned about every facet of your life. He knows your every move, thought, weakness and strength and He loves you anyway. He has numbered the hairs on your head and has collected every tear that you've shed. He wakes you up every morning, stays with you all day and protects you all night. He's just that into you. He wants to talk to you every day. He loves just to hear your voice. Spending time with you is His greatest joy. He's just that into you. He came to earth, was born and died so you could live with Him forever. He did it just to show you how much He loves you. He's just that into you. If you don't know of whom I speak, let me introduce you to Jesus Christ, the person who is the most into you. If you already know Him, draw closer to Him. If you've gone astray, He welcomes you back to Him with open arms. He's just that into you.

Prayer

Father we thank you for care about every facet of our lives. We don't deserve your love or care but, you love us in spite of us. Everyday help us to love and appreciate you more and learn to care about others.
In Jesus' name I pray. Amen.

Prayer Concerns

Create a "thank you list" to God for His love for you. He's into you. Are you into Him?

He's Just that into You!

Journal/Reflect/Strategize

He's Just that into You!

"The quality of your life is the quality of your relationships." Anthony Robbins

But God demonstrates his own love for us in this: While we were still sinners, Christ died for us.
Romans 5:8 (NIV)

For we do not have a High Priest Who is unable to understand and sympathize and have a shared feeling with our weaknesses and infirmities and liability to the assaults of temptation, but One Who has been tempted in every respect as we are, yet without sinning.
Hebrews 4:15 (The Amplified)

Casting all your care upon him; for he careth for you. I Peter 5:7 (KJV)

Devotional Objective:
God loves you and everything that concerns you. He came to earth in the form of Jesus Christ, died and rose again just for you. Are you "into" God in return? What have you done for Him lately? What are you doing for others?

Materials Needed
Everyday Miracles Book
Holy Bible (version of your choice)
Everyday Miracles Music CD
Worksheet Into1
Box (es) of inspirational cards enough for the entire group to have two each.
Dictionary of your choice

Vocabulary
Love
Care
Demonstration

Opening Activity:
Open with prayer. Allow time for celebrations, announcements and prayer concerns. Read the devotional and prayer entitled, He's Just that Into You (Page 41 of the Everyday Miracles book), and record any prayer concerns. (Music can be played during opening activity.) Share any thoughts regarding the scripture, devotional or prayer.

Questions to guide discussion: God is concerned with us but, we should also be concerned about what God is concerned about. For example, we should be concerned about the lost, the widow, the fatherless, the imprisoned and the sick. How do you reach out to others? Are you more concerned about your own needs rather than the needs of others?

Activities:
Activity #1 – Complete Part 1 of Worksheet Into1.

Discussion: What does the phrase "he's into to you" mean to you? Have you ever had someone that was really "into" you? How did that make you feel? What did they do to make you feel this way? Do you know that God is into every aspect about you, what you love and what you are concerned about? What are some areas of concern that you have in your life?

Sharing: Complete Part 2 of the Worksheet Into1. Allow time for discussion and sharing. Allow time for discussion and sharing.

Activity #2 – God is concerned about you but, He is also concerned about others. In Part 3 of the Worksheet Into1, there is an area for you to write the names of two people that you are concerned about. Additionally, there are inspirational cards that you can write a note of encouragement. Even if you don't have a mailing address for them, complete the inside card and prepare it for mailing.

Discussion: How did writing the card make you feel? How do you think the person will feel once they receive the card?

Sharing: Allow time for this activity and discussion at its completion.

Response/Share/Journal
Respond: How do you feel about God's concern for you? Do you have a greater awareness of God's concern for you or did you know it all along and this lesson was a reminder?

Share: Allow time for discussion of the responses.

Journal: Play the song "Journey" on the Everyday Miracles Music CD and give time for journaling about He's Just that Into You. (Note: If someone has difficulty with things to journal about, feel free to ask the questions for consideration.)

Closing activity, thoughts and prayer
Closing Thoughts and Prayer: Remind the group that God is concerned about everything that concerns you. Additionally, God is concerned about and taking care of the entire universe. Reaching out to someone in need or in crisis is God working through you to help something that He is concerned about. Offer prayer for all prayer concerns including those listed on the Worksheet Into1 that was shared and some not mentioned. Pray that each group member will be strengthened, guided and assured that God has chosen and will equip them.

Extension Activity: In the next week, find a person, issue or organization that you can assist. This could be volunteer your time, give of your finances or assist the organization or person in some other way.

Follow-up Activity and Resources
- Read the next or assigned devotional prior to the next meeting time,
- Listen to music provided on the Everyday Miracles music CDs,
- Read 2 Kings 4:1-7,
- At the next meeting, allow opportunity for sharing and or testimony as a follow-up on their progress of the "He's Just that Into You" Lesson.

He's Just that Into You!

Part 1: What does it mean to you for someone to be "into you"? How does that make you feel?

****
Part 2: List some areas of concern that you have in your life?

****
Part 3: List at least two people that you are concerned about.

Worksheet—Into1

Launch Out Into the Deep

Are You Ready to Launch?

"When He had stopped speaking, He said to Simon, Launch out into the deep and let down your nets for a catch." Luke 5:4 (KJV)

Launch

Peter was a fisherman. He has a great reputation and a thriving business catching fish. In Luke, Peter had been fishing all night and caught nothing. Jesus a carpenter, says said, "Launch out into the deep and let down your nets for a catch." Because Peter trusted Jesus, he obeyed. He launched out into the deep and caught a great catch of fish. Peter caught so many fish, he had to call his partners for help and filled a second boat. The bible says that both boats were so full that they began to sink. Have you ever taken a big risk and won? You were unsure of the result but, willing to go for it anyway? If you took a risk with a person or on a project that you had limited knowledge of, what about taking a risk with God? As we grow in our spiritual relationship, God will ask us to launch out into the deep water of this life. The deep is the unknown, unchartered territory outside of our comfort zone. One day you may find yourself in a new job, a new call in ministry or a new city. For you, that may be launching into the deep. You haven't a clue what could or will happen but, know this, that Jesus is right there with you to help you.

At the end of the story, Peter ran and fell down at Jesus' feet in appreciation and humility. Jesus had increased Peter's faith, his business and their relationship. Remember Jesus is concerned about every aspect of your life. He wants to prosper you in mind, body and spirit. Trust God and launch out into the deep!

Prayer

Father we thank you that you love us and we can trust you. You know what's best for us. So be with us when you lead us into unfamiliar territory. Lead, love and launch us into the deep waters of life. In Jesus' Name I pray. Amen.

Prayer Concerns

_____
_____
_____
_____
_____
_____
_____
_____
_____
_____
_____
_____
_____
_____
_____
_____

Have you launched into the deep waters of life or are you standing on the shore watching your life go by? What are you waiting on? Launch!

Launch

Journal/Reflect/Strategize

Launch

"Progress always involves risks. You can't steal second base and keep your foot on first."
Frederick B. Wilcox

"A ship is safe in harbor, but that's not what ships are for." William Shedd

"If You Want to Walk on Water, You've Got to Get Out of the Boat" – John Ortberg

"In order to get something you've never had, you have to do something you've never done." Anonymous

Devotional Objective: There are times that God will lead us into unfamiliar territory and/or command you to do something outside of your comfort zone. Do you trust God enough to get out of your comfort zone and launch out in the deep? Get ready to launch.

Materials Needed
Everyday Miracles Book
Holy Bible (version of your choice)
Everyday Miracles Music CD
Worksheet Deep1
Dictionary of your choice

Vocabulary
Launch
Unfamiliar
Trust
Risk
Reputation

Opening Activity: Open with prayer. Allow time for celebrations, announcements and prayer concerns. Read the devotional and prayer entitled, Launch Out into the Deep (Page 45 of the Everyday Miracles book), and put in writing any prayer concerns. (Music can be played during opening activity.) Share any thoughts regarding the scripture, devotional or prayer.

Questions to guide discussion: Do you trust God? How much? Are you more afraid of failing or losing your reputation? Are you a risk taker? What are you willing to risk for God? What are you willing to risk to obtain your purpose?

Activities:
Activity #1 – Each group member should have a copy of Worksheet Deep1. Individually, each group member should answer part 1 of Worksheet Deep1.

Sharing: Group members should be divided into pairs to explain their answer in Part of the Worksheet Deep1. The facilitator should name the items on the list and find out how the group members rated the items in Part 1 by raising their hands. (For example, all those who rated Family as number 5 raise your hands.)

Discussion: Allow time for discussion in a small group or in the large group.

Activity #2—Each group member should complete Part 2 and Part 3 of Worksheet Deep1 individually.

Sharing/Discussion: Allow time for discussion in a small group or in the large group.

Respond/Share/Journal
Respond: If God is speaking to you about launching into the deep in your career or ministry, how are you going to prepare yourself? Peter had to call his partners for help to collect all of the fish after he launched out into the deep and obeyed Jesus. What do you think you will need from Him and others to complete this project? Do you have any helpers, team members or partners that you trust? Do you need God to send quality, trustworthy people to help you?

Share: Allow time for discussion in a small group or in the large group.

Journal: Play the song "Follow Me" on the Everyday Miracles Music CD and give time for journaling about Launch Out in the Deep. (Note: If someone has difficulty with things to journal about, feel free to ask the questions to guide discussion.)

Closing activity, thoughts and prayer:
Closing Thoughts and Prayer: Launching into the deep or unchartered territory can be scary and intimidating. Know that God is with you and calls those who are willing to take huge steps of faith for Him. Pray for those who have daunting undertakings or are making critical decisions in their walk with God. Pray that each group member will be strengthened, guided and assured that God has chosen and will equip them.

Follow-up Activity and Resources
- Read the next or assigned devotional prior to the next meeting time.
- Listen to music provided on the Everyday Miracles music CDs.
- Read Deuteronomy 28th Chapter.
- At the next meeting, allow opportunity for sharing and or testimony as a follow-up on their progress of the "Launch Out in the Deep" Lesson.

Launch Out into the Deep

Part 1:

Rate the following between 1-5 with the number 5 being the most important.

_____Family
_____Reputation/Character
_____Business
_____Friends
_____Faith/Spirituality

Part 2:

On the list of five items in Part 1, what are you willing to risk to fulfill the purpose of God in your life?

On the list of five items in Part 1, what are you not willing to risk to fulfill the purpose of God in your life?

Part 3:

How much do you trust God?

Worksheet—Deep1

Legacy

What Will Be Your Life's Legacy?

"A GOOD name is rather to be chosen than great riches, and loving favour rather than silver and gold." Proverbs 22:1 (KJV)

Legacy

People are living longer today than ever before. The knowledge gained through modern technology, medicine and physical fitness has literally prolonged some people's lives. If you practice good eating habits and receive preventative medical care, you could live a long time. How do you want to be remembered? Truthfully, what will people say about you when you are dead? What type of legacy will you leave behind? Proverbs tells us that a good name should be chosen over great riches. You can chase after riches and people may envy you but, how did you treat others while acquiring your riches? Having a good name includes how you treat people you know and don't know. A good name and reputation is the result of handling your business, social and spiritual affairs correctly. People all make mistakes but, to have a good name and reputation you correct mistakes, make adjustments and change incorrect behavior. Alzheimer's and dementia take your memory, alter your personality and thus, change your behavior. If you develop this disease, people will make allowances and adjustments for your behavior. But, without a cause or disease, are you just mean, hurtful and cruel to people? Do you make people feel better when you show up or do people recoil at the mention of your name? Thousands of years after His ascension, we are still talking about the miracles, works and sayings of Jesus. He had such a great impact on the world that people are still getting to know and believe in Him today. He left a great legacy. What will be yours?

Prayer

Father we thank you for this day and the opportunity that we have to influence our world. You gave us an example of love and how we should impact the world around us. Help us to leave a legacy of love, kindness and righteousness. In Jesus' name I pray. Amen.

Prayer Concerns

What will be your legacy? Share it with a friend.

Legacy

Journal/Reflect/Strategize

By faith Enoch was translated that he should not see death; and was not found, because God had translated him: for before his translation he had this testimony, that he pleased God.
Hebrews 11:5 (KJV)

"The purpose of life is a life of purpose." Robert Byrne

"When I stand before God at the end of my life, I would hope that I would not have a single bit of talent left, and could say, "I used everything you gave me". Erma Bombeck

Devotional Objective: Each one of our lives is important. How you live your life does have an impact on someone else. Whether you know it or not, you will leave a legacy after you have departed this life. What will that legacy look like?

Materials Needed
Everyday Miracles Book
Holy Bible
Everyday Miracles Music CD
Thematic or specialty paper enough for each group member
Worksheet Legacy1
Dictionary

Vocabulary
Legacy
Impact
Purpose

Opening Activity: Open with prayer. Allow time for celebrations, announcements and prayer concerns. Read the devotional and prayer entitled, Legacy (Page 49 of the Everyday Miracles book), and jot down any prayer concerns. (Music can be played during opening activity.) Share any thoughts regarding the scripture, devotional or prayer.

Questions for Consideration: What does the word legacy mean to you? What do you want to leave as your life's legacy?

Activities:
Activity #1: In this activity, each group member should have Worksheet Legacy1. In Part 1 of the worksheet, each group member should imagine that they are now deceased and write how they would like to be remembered. (Note: remind the group that this is not to be considered a morbid exercise about death but, more about the direction and effectiveness of their life.)

Discussion: Based on what you wrote in Part 1, have you lived a full life so far? Do you live only for yourself or do you allow time for others?

Part 2 of the worksheet should be completed individually and discussion should be considered if the group feels comfortable.

Share: Allow time for discussion in a small group or in the large group.

Activity #2: If there is time, give each group member a piece of specialty paper you provide, and they should write out their own obituary. Because the group members are still alive, the date of death is left blank. (Note: if the group members are more seasoned or are more elderly, remind them that this could be a part of an estate planning exercise.)

Respond/Share/Journal
Response: How did this exercise make you feel? Are you having an impact on an organization, church, company or someone's life? Will you be making any changes in your life based on these activities?

Share: Allow time for discussion in a small group or in the large group.

Journal: Play a song from the Everyday Miracles Music CD and give time for journaling about Legacy. (Note: If someone has difficulty with things to journal about, feel free to ask the questions to guide discussion.)

Closing activity, thoughts and prayer
Closing Thoughts and Prayer: Jesus Christ left us a great legacy of healing, love and power. With the Holy Spirit in us, we should seek to leave a positive and powerful legacy for the people around us. What legacy will you leave behind? Pray that each group member will be strengthened, guided and assured that God has chosen and will equip them.

Extension Activity: A part of leaving a great legacy is making sure that your family and your personal affairs are in order in case of your untimely death. Do you have a final will and living will? Do you have enough insurance and savings to cover medical, burial or other financial obligations? If something happened to you, is there anyone you know and trust who can handle your affairs? If it is available and there is time, bring in a life insurance agent or attorney who specializes in estate planning to offer guidance and answer any questions of the group members.

Follow-up Activity and Resources
- Read the next or assigned devotional prior to the next meeting time.
- Listen to music provided on the Everyday Miracles music CDs.
- Read 2 Timothy 4 (entire chapter).
- At the next meeting, allow opportunity for sharing and or testimony as a follow-up on their progress of the "Legacy" Lesson.

Part 1: Write down how you want to be remembered? To what person, company, organization or church have you made a substantial contribution?

Part 2: Is there any unfinished business? Is there someone you need to contact or a project that needs to be completed?

Worksheet—Legacy1

Make Room for Jesus

SCHEDULE

Is Jesus Your Top Priority?

"And she brought forth her firstborn son, and wrapped him in swaddling clothes, and laid him in a manger; because there was no room for them in the inn."
Luke 2:7 (KJV)

Make Room for Jesus

Cleaning out your closets, cabinets, and cars is necessary because they become filled with trash, clutter or unessential items. Additionally, when you have accumulated so much unnecessary stuff, you don't have room for anything new. Maybe you just can't find the things that you do need because they are hidden. For hundreds of years, the children of Israel prayed for the Messiah to come and set up a Kingdom on earth. The prophecy of old was told from generation to generation so that it would not be forgotten or missed. But, Jesus the Messiah was born in a stable. The announcement of his birth was only told to a few shepherds while keeping their sheep outside at night. There was no room for Jesus in the inn. There was a crowd in town because it was time to pay annual taxes. There were no room reservations made for Mary to give birth to Jesus. Can you imagine waiting, praying and begging for something more than 400 years and missing it because you didn't have room? I wonder if the inn keeper had known that the King of Kings was to be born that night, would he have given up his bed for Mary to give birth to Jesus? Are you willing to give up some of your comforts to make room for Jesus? Because there was no room for Jesus in the inn, the masses missed the light show of the stars, the appearance of the heavenly angels and the personal invitation to see the fulfillment of prophecy of Jesus lying in the manger. There was no room for Jesus. Have you made room for Jesus in your life?

Does He have a seat, a room and enough closet space in your life to stay awhile?

Does He have a designated portion of your day to hear your voice speaking love, thanksgiving and praise to Him? Do you allow Him to interrupt your schedule, determine your destiny or guide your decision making? Will you allow Him to give you goals, optimize your objectives and counsel your career? Clear your calendar. Throw away the trash. Move away from the mundane and make room for Jesus. He has great plans in store for you. He is making room for you to live with Him forever. Make room for Jesus.

Prayer

Prayer: Father I thank you that you loved me enough to come down from Heaven, live on earth, die a horrible death and rise to give me eternal life. For this I say thank you. You are the King of my life and I give you free course, headship and control of my life. In Jesus' name I pray. Amen.

Prayer Concerns

How important is Jesus in your life?

Make Room for Jesus

Journal/Reflect/Strategize

Make Room for Jesus

And she brought forth her firstborn son, and wrapped him in swaddling clothes, and laid him in a manger; because there was no room for them in the inn. Luke 2:7 (KJV)

Devotional Objective: To understand the importance of keeping Jesus as the leader and top priority in your daily life.

Materials Needed
Everyday Miracles Book
Holy Bible
Everyday Miracles Music CD
Worksheet Make1 and Worksheet Make2
Dictionary

Vocabulary
Priorities
Value
Importance

Opening Activity: Open with prayer. Allow time for celebrations, announcements and prayer concerns. Read the devotional and prayer entitled, Make Room for Jesus (Page 53 of the Everyday Miracles book), and write down any prayer concerns. (Music can be played during opening activity.) Share any thoughts regarding the scripture, devotional or prayer.

    Questions for Consideration: Where is Jesus on your list of priorities? Do you have him a part of your everyday life? Do you make special time for Jesus? How much do you value your relationship with Him?

Activities:
    Activity #1: Each group member should receive and complete the Worksheet Make1. The values should be ranked from 1 to 10 with 1 being the highest or most important.
    Share: Group members should be divided into pairs to share individual selections from Worksheet Make1.
    Discussion: Allow time for discussion about how the group members ranked each value.

Activity #2: Each group member should receive and complete Worksheet Make2.

Discussion: How does your daily schedule look? Is your schedule filled to capacity or are there open times for Jesus?

Respond/Share/Journal

Respond: How did this exercise make you feel? After looking at your schedule, are there places you need to make adjustments to make time for Jesus?

Share: Allow time to share responses in a small or large.

Journal: Play a song from the Everyday Miracles Music CD and give time for journaling about "Make Room for Jesus". (Note: If someone has difficulty with things to journal about, feel free to ask the questions to guide discussion.)

Closing activity, thoughts and prayer

Closing Thoughts and Prayer: Making room for Jesus in your daily life will help you stay on the course to destiny. Open your heart and adjust your schedule to make more time and room for Jesus. He has great plans for your life. Let Him lead the way. Pray that each group member will be strengthened, guided and assured that God has chosen and will equip them.

Extension Activity: Give each group member an additional copy of Worksheet Make2. Ask them to make a new daily schedule which allows for more time for study and meditation with God as homework. At the next group meeting, compare the first worksheet Make2 and the one each group member completed for homework. How has the schedule changed? What spiritual improvements do you think will be made as a result of the schedule changes?

Follow-up Activity and Resources:
- Read the next or assigned devotional prior to the next meeting time
- Listen to music provided on the Everyday Miracles music CDs
- Read Daniel 6:10; John 4:21-24; Psalm 34; Psalm 91
- At the meeting, allow opportunity for sharing and or testimony as a follow-up on their progress of the "Make Room for Jesus" Lesson.

Make Room for Jesus

On a scale from 1 to 10, rank the following values with 1 being the highest or most important.

_____Employment

_____Friends

_____Family

_____Religion/God

_____Material Possessions

_____Church

_____Education

_____Peace

_____Love

_____Conflict

Worksheet—Make1

Make Room for Jesus

Write down your daily schedule. (Note: pick the busiest day of the week)

Day of the Week_____

Morning

Noon

Night

Looking at the above schedule. When did you make time for Jesus? What changes in your schedule need to be made?

Worksheet—Make2

Mentorship

Me, A Mentor?

"...Then he arose and followed Elijah, and became his servant."
I Kings 19:21 (KJV)

Mentorship

In the bible there are numerous examples of leadership by mentorship. We see how one on one, patient teaching and instruction can produce Godly leaders. For example, Elijah mentored Elisha, Eli taught Samuel, Samuel anointed David, Paul taught and mentored Timothy. Jesus called, mentored, taught and empowered his disciples. The older, more experienced men were able to recognize the gifts in others. They would take on the responsibility of encouraging, developing and imparting knowledge into the younger inexperienced men. Everyone can not lead a leader. Some people see the gifting in others and seek to destroy or control the gift. Such is the relationship of Saul and David. The relationship began well but, ended in David running for his life because Saul was trying to kill him. God, however, intended that each person's gift would be developed, matured and celebrated. With just three years of intense mentoring, Jesus' disciples turned the world upside down. Who are the people of great gifting that God has placed in your life? Are these people filled with purpose that needs your encouragement? Ask God to open your eyes and create an opportunity to help someone's gift to increase and blossom. Remember that there are gifts inside of you. These gifts can be released, enlarged and expanded for God's Glory through mentorship.

Prayer

Father, I thank you for the family of God. Each part of the body of Christ is important and necessary for the building of the Kingdom of God. Give us wisdom and knowledge to build and encourage each other to be stronger, to live the abundant life. Help me to mentor someone so they can be all that You called them to be. In Jesus' name I pray. Amen.

Prayer Concerns

What makes a good mentor?

Mentorship

Journal/Reflect/Strategize

Mentorship

"Better ask ten times than go astray once." Yiddish Saying

"A good objective of leadership is to help those who are doing poorly to do well and to help those who are doing well to do even better." Jim Rohn

"Leaders don't create followers, they create more leaders." Tom Peters

Devotional Objective: To be introduced to or discover the value of mentorship. Mentoring is designed to help develop, encourage and further a person's gift, ministry or business. Are you a mentor?

Materials Needed
Everyday Miracles Book
Everyday Miracles Music CD
Holy Bible (version of your choice)
Wrapped gift box or decorative gift bag
3 x 5 index cards
Worksheet – Mentor1

Vocabulary
Gifted
Mentoring
Impartation
Enrichment
Development

Opening Activity: Open with prayer. Allow time for celebrations, announcements and prayer concerns. Read the devotional and prayer entitled, Mentorship (Page 59 of the Everyday Miracles book), and write down any prayer concerns. (Music can be played during opening activity.) Share any thoughts regarding the scripture, devotional or prayer.

    Questions for Consideration: Is there a gift of a person that God has placed in your life to assist you and/or to receive impartation, enrichment and development from you? Do you need to be mentored by someone to assist you in fulfilling your dreams and reach your destiny? Have you ever had a mentor? What does mentorship mean to you? What makes a good mentor? What makes a bad mentor?

Activities:

Activity #1: Open Discussion. Show the gift wrapped box or gift bag to the group members. Ask them how they would handle this gift if they knew a 7 carat diamond or a crystal vase were located inside.

Discussion/Sharing: Do you think people are a gift from God? How should God's creation be treated? Do we have a Christian obligation to mentor people? What is so hard or easy about mentoring someone? What makes a good or bad mentor? Why do you think it is difficult to find good mentors?

Activity #2: Exercise in mentorship. There is a list of possible tasks that can be done during a group meeting. Prior to the session, write one of these tasks on a 3 x 5 index card. There should be enough cards for every 2 group members to complete. The following are some examples however, you may think of others:

Show me how to tie my shoes
Show me how to tie a neck tie
Show me how to thread a needle
Show me how to get to the bathroom in the building.

Respond/Share/Journal

Respond: What did you learn from both group activities? Do you think your partner in activity #2 would make a good mentor? Why or why not? Would you make a good mentor? Could you help someone achieve without placing yourself in the way? Do you need a mentor to help you get to your next level and fulfill your purpose? Are you ready for a mentor? Are you ready to be a mentor? Why or why not?

Share: Allow time to share responses in a small or large.

Journal: Play the song "Teach Me" from the Everyday Miracles Music CD and give time for journaling about Mentorship. (Note: If someone has difficulty with things to journal about, feel free to ask the questions to guide discussion.)

Closing activity, thoughts and prayer

Closing Thoughts and Prayer: Mentoring is more than just telling someone what to do. The objective of mentoring is to be a guide, provide encouragement, impart wisdom and to lead others by example rather than being a dictator. Additionally, a Christian mentor should be in constant prayer about what to say, when to say or how to say anything to their mentee. The purpose is for the mentee to grow, develop and become all that God intended for them to be and not just what you, the mentor, thinks they should be.

Pray that each group member will be strengthened, guided and assured that God has chosen and will equip them.

Extension Activity: The following is a list of websites that provide additional information regarding Christian mentoring programs and how to effectively establish them in your organization or study group.

- Christian Mentorship: http://www.christianmentors.org/
- Faith centered mentoring and more:
- http://www.faithmentoringandmore.com/html/articles/idea_20.htm
- How to develop a mentoring program? http://www.intothyword.org/apps/articles/default.asp?articleid=42724&columnid=3844
- How to start a mentorship program? http://www.bnet.com/2403-13058_23-212133.html

Follow-up Activity and Resources
- Read the next or assigned devotional prior to the next meeting time
- Listen to music provided on the Everyday Miracles music CDs
- Read I Timothy 6; Titus 2
- At the meeting, allow opportunity for sharing and or testimony as a follow-up on their progress of the "Mentorship" Lesson.

Mentorship

What makes a good mentor?

Are you mentoring anyone? How?

Do you have a mentor? Who are they and how are they helping you?

Worksheet—Mentor1

New Place

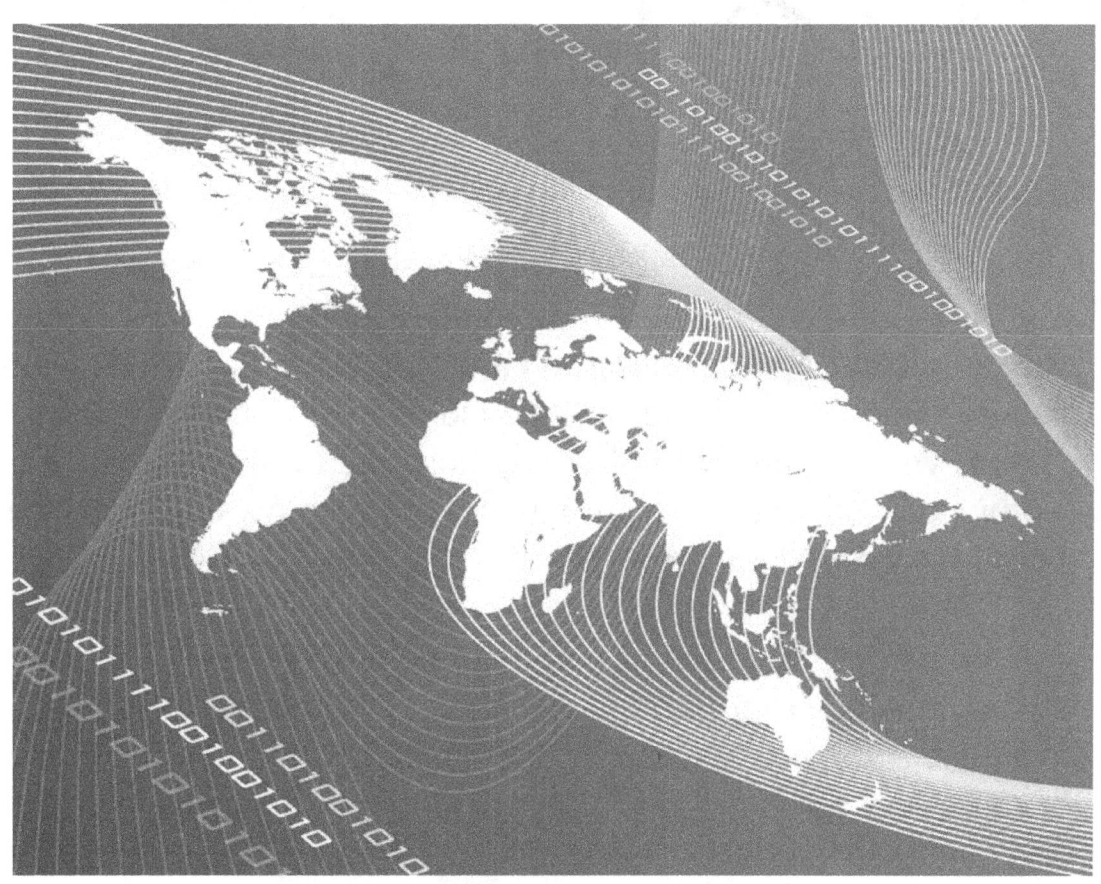

Will You Follow Where He Leads?

"Now the LORD had said unto Abram, Get thee out of thy country, and from thy kindred, and from thy father's house, unto a land that I will shew thee."
Genesis 12:1 (KJV)

A New Place

My husband and I were invited to his co-worker's Christmas party. The food was wonderful and the house was impeccably decorated. I knew very few people but, I was willing to enjoy the evening with my husband and be sociable. So I smiled, nodded, ate from the buffet and shook hands with all those to whom my husband introduced me. to. Once I adjusted to the new surroundings, I enjoyed myself immensely with the new people, in the new place.

Have you ever felt God drawing you to some new places, new people and new positions in your life? In the text, Abraham received a blessing, a promise and a new name. He then became the father of many nations because he was willing to follow God to a new place. His obedience was counted as righteousness and consequently, the entire nation of Israel inherited benefits, privileges and blessings through his faith. What assignment might you fulfill in the new place? What person, group of people or nation is waiting to be blessed by you in the new place? God desires to take you some new places physically and spiritually. Like Abraham, are you willing to say yes and follow God even to a place you've never been? In a new place with God is always the right place. Follow God everyday to the new places He has for you. You may be surprised at the great things He will show, do and work through you in the New Place.

Prayer

Father we thank you for the new places that you are taking me. Help me to trust and follow you wholeheartedly. In Jesus' name I pray. Amen.

Prayer Concerns

_____
_____
_____
_____
_____
_____
_____
_____
_____
_____
_____
_____
_____
_____
_____
_____

What have you learned in the new places?

A New Place

Journal/Reflect/Strategize

New Place

"…..lead the people unto the place of which I have spoken unto thee….." Exodus 32:34 (KJV)

"Every morning is a fresh beginning. Every day is the world made new. Today is a new day. Today is my world made new. I have lived all my life up to this moment, to come to this day. This moment--this day--is as good as any moment in all eternity. I shall make of this day--each moment of this day--a heaven on earth. This is my day of opportunity." Dan Custer

I will lead the blind by ways they have not known, along unfamiliar paths I will guide them; I will turn the darkness into light before them and make the rough places smooth. These are the things I will do; I will not forsake them. Isaiah 42:16 (KJV)

Devotional Objective: God wants to lead you to some new places for physical and spiritual growth. God's ways are not our ways but, His plan might be to create a new better you in a new place.

Materials Needed
Everyday Miracles Book
Everyday Miracles Music CD
Holy Bible (version of your choice)
Worksheet – Place1

Vocabulary
Lead
Follow
Place
Growth
Comfort zone

Opening Activity: Open with prayer. Allow time for celebrations, announcements and prayer concerns. Read the devotional and prayer entitled, New Place (Page 63 in the Everyday Miracles book), and write down any prayer concerns. (Music can be played during opening activity.) Share any thoughts regarding the scripture, devotional or prayer.

Questions for consideration: How did it feel to move away from home for the first time? Were you nervous, anxious or did you adjust right away? Ask the group what it felt like the first night they slept in their dorm room or new apartment after just moving in?

Activities:

Activity #1: Each group member should receive and complete Worksheet Place1 individually.

Sharing: Allow time for sharing with a partner the answers and thoughts completed on Worksheet Place1.

Discussion: Open discussion to the entire group. Facilitate the group discussion with any additional questions or issues that may arise regarding being lead into a new place. If necessary, revisit the devotional and the story of Abraham found in Genesis 12. Remind the group of how he was lead by God from his hometown, his culture and family to a new place that only God would show him.

Respond/Share/Journal

Respond: After completing the activity, are you in a new place? Do feel God leading you in a different direction? How does this new place feel?

Share: Allow time to share responses in a small or large.

Journal: Play the song "Journey" from the Everyday Miracles Music CD and give time for journaling about New Place. (Note: If someone has difficulty with things to journal about, feel free to ask the questions to guide discussion.)

Closing activity, thoughts and prayer

Closing Thoughts and Prayer: God has great things in store for you. There may be some new places that you will have to visit to experience and receive the things and fulfill the plans He has for your life. Are you willing to follow where He leads? Are you willing to give up some people, places and positions for the new "God" places? Pray that each group member will be strengthened, guided and assured that God has chosen and will equip them.

Extension Activity: Ask each group member to visit a new restaurant or new retail store. How did it feel? How did you act in the new restaurant or new store? Report on your responses at the next group meeting session.

Follow-up Activity and Resources

- Read the next or assigned devotional prior to the next meeting time
- Listen to music provided on the Everyday Miracles music CDs
- Read Exodus 15:13; Psalm 31:3; Psalm 63:8; Proverbs 4:11;
- At the meeting, allow opportunity for sharing and or testimony as a follow-up on their progress of the "New Place" Lesson.

New Place

Have you ever visited a place for the first time? How did it feel? How did you feel? Did you compare it to others places that you have been before? Do you like going to new places for the first time or would you prefer to repeat visiting the same places repeatedly? Write your answers and additional thoughts below.

What if God suddenly moved your entire family to a new state, new city, new job, new home and new church? How would you feel? How would you adjust? Write down your answers and additional thoughts.

Worksheet—Place1

Purpose-Filled Life

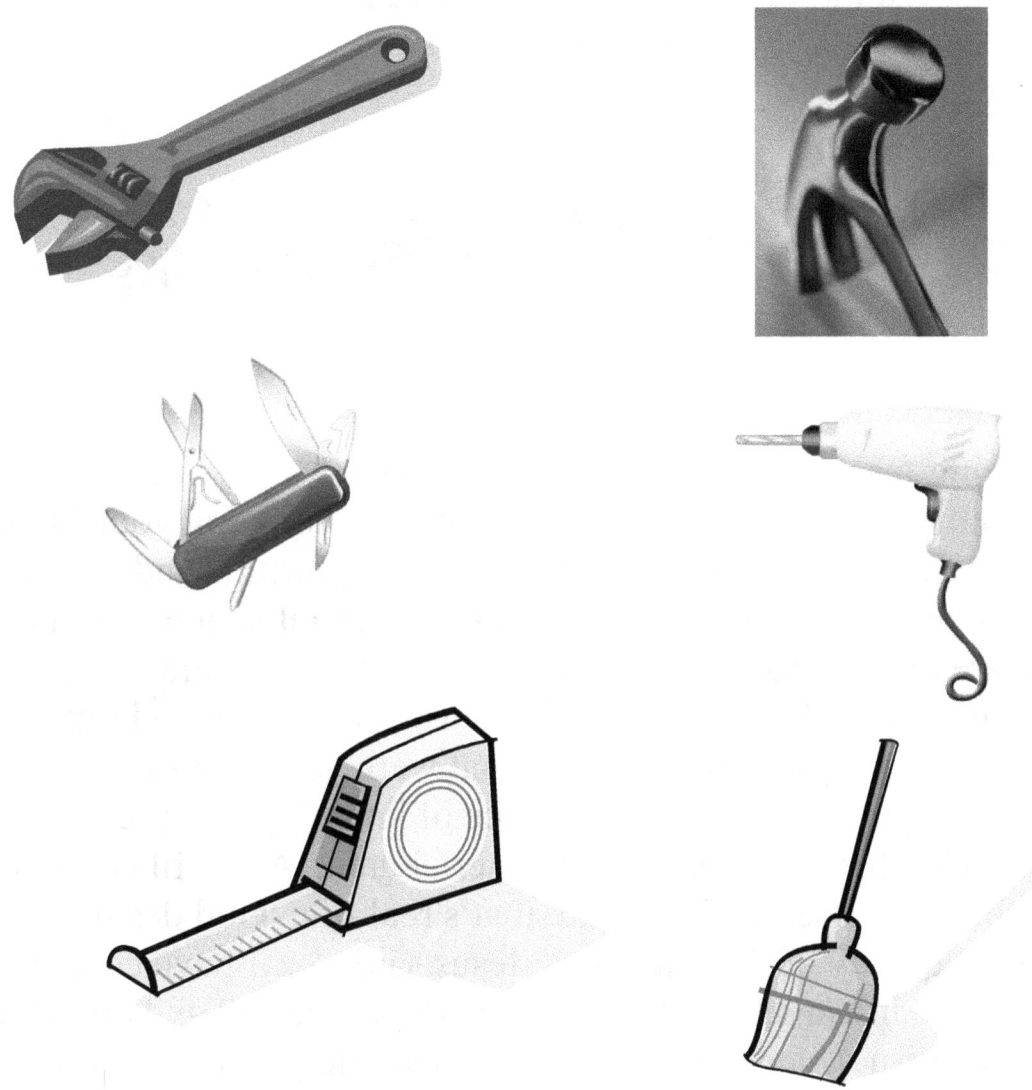

Are You Fulfilling Your God-Given Purpose?

"I am come that they might have life, and that they might have it more abundantly." John 10:10 (KJV)

"Many are the plans in a man's heart, but it is the LORD's purpose that prevails." Proverbs 19:21 (NIV)

"...To this end was I born, and for this cause came I into the world...." John 18:37 (KJV)

Purpose Filled Life

Are you living for another car, house or promotion on your job? Do you find yourself working harder and harder but, enjoying your life less and less. Society places great emphasis on fame, fortune and financial wealth. The accomplishments are spotlighted, imitated and emulated but, these are all external signs of success. That is what the world teaches. What about the purpose of God for which you were born? What is your purpose on this earth? What were you born to do? When this life is over you should have the peace of knowing that you lived a life worth living for God and not for material gain. A life filled with meaning for a purpose that is eternal, that's real life. God desires to give you that quality of life each day. Jesus said, "....I have come that you might have life and that more abundantly, to the full and overflowing." Sure, pursue your dreams, get an education, go to the top of your career field, be the best you, you can be. But, put no eternal hope in any of these things. You should put your hope in God and live for Him and He will take you places that you can only imagine. No matter what you do and accomplish, make sure to live the purpose filled life!

Prayer

Lord we thank you for this day and another opportunity to live our lives filled with and on purpose. Lead and guide us to the life we were born to live. In Jesus' name I pray. Amen.

Prayer Concerns

_____
_____
_____
_____
_____
_____
_____
_____
_____
_____
_____
_____
_____
_____
_____

Are you living the purpose filled life?

Purpose Filled Life

Journal/Reflect/Strategize

Purpose Filled Life

"...To this end was I born, and for this cause came I into the world...." John 18:37 (KJV)

Devotional Objective: Living the abundant life is one that involves living a life filled with and for God's purpose.

Materials Needed
Everyday Miracles Book
3-5 small objects, e.g. flash light, spoon, CD player, paper clip, pen/pencil, etc.
Everyday Miracles Music CD
Holy Bible (version of your choice)
Worksheet – Purpose1

Vocabulary
Purpose
Living
Abundant
Fulfilled

Opening Activity: Open with prayer. Allow time for celebrations, announcements and prayer concerns. Read the devotional and prayer entitled, Purpose Filled Life (Page 67 in the Everyday Miracles book), and write down any prayer concerns. (Music can be played during opening activity.) Share any thoughts regarding the scripture, devotional or prayer.

   Questions for Consideration: What is your God given purpose? Do you know the reason why you were born? Do you ever feel like there is something missing in your life?

Activities:
   Activity #1 – Each group member should receive a copy of Worksheet Purpose1. The facilitator should display the small objects to the group one by one. Once the group members see the object they should write the purpose or use of the object.
   Discussion: Can the object be used for anything else? Is the object often misused or not used to fulfill its proper purpose?

Activity #2 – Each group member should have a copy and individually complete Worksheet Purpose2. Allow time for discussion. (Suggestion: if the group is relatively small, open up the discussion to the entire group.

Share: If the group is relatively large, divide the group in pairs or groups of 3 for discussion.)

Discussion: Do we definitely know what our purpose is? If we do know our purpose, are we fulfilling it? If we do not know what our purpose is on the earth, are we asking God or wandering aimlessly?

Respond/Share/Journal

Respond: After completing the two activities, are you living a purpose filled life?

Share: Allow time to share responses in a small or large group.

Journal: Play the song "Love and Choose You" from the Everyday Miracles Music CD and give time for journaling about a Purpose Filled Life. (Note: If someone has difficulty with things to journal about, feel free to ask the questions to guide discussion.)

Closing activity, thoughts and prayer

Closing Thoughts and Prayer: Jesus came to earth to fulfill one purpose and that is to redeem mankind of the penalty of sin. He did so through his death on the cross, burial and resurrection. What were you born to do on this earth? Fulfilling our purpose on earth is a key element to the abundant life that God came and died to give each of us. Look at your life right now and assess whether it is a purpose filled or a duty filled life. Pray that each group member will be strengthened, guided and assured that God has chosen and will equip them.

Extension Activity: If you don't know what your purpose is, ask God this week. If you do know what your purpose is, ask God to give direction in fulfilling your purpose.

Follow-up Activity and Resources

- Read the next or assigned devotional prior to the next meeting time
- Listen to music provided on the Everyday Miracles music CDs
- Read: Ecclesiastes 3; Isaiah 14
- At the next meeting, allow opportunity for sharing and or testimony as a follow-up on their progress of the "Purpose Filled Life" Lesson.

Purpose-Filled Life

What is the object's purpose?

Object #1
_____
_____
_____

Object #2
_____
_____
_____

Object #3
_____
_____
_____

Object #4
_____
_____
_____

Object #5
_____
_____
_____

Have you ever used any of the objects for another purpose?

Worksheet—Purpose 1

Purpose-Filled Life

Do you know what your God given purpose is? If you don't know quite what your purpose is, what do you feel God is calling or leading you to do? If you know what your purpose is, what actions are you taking to fulfill that purpose? Are you helping anyone else fulfill their purpose? Write your answers and thoughts below.

_____
_____
_____
_____
_____
_____
_____
_____
_____
_____
_____
_____
_____
_____
_____
_____
_____
_____
_____
_____
_____
_____
_____
_____
_____
_____
_____
_____
_____

Worksheet—Purpose2

Restoration

Are You Ready to Be Restored?

"He restoreth my soul." Psalm 23: (KJV)

Restoration

Have you ever had a computer crash? A virus attacks your computer and your data is lost forever? There is much frustration. Time and money are spent to get your computer fixed. But, there is a CD sent with the new computer that should be kept in a safe place called a restore or recovery CD. With this CD, your computer can be restored to its original default state. This does not ensure that you will not lose data or need to re-install software but, the actual computer can be restored. Wouldn't that be nice to put a CD inside of us? That CD could restore our soul when we suffered a crash in spirit. It could restore our broken relationships. Maybe it could restore to us the time and effort that we have lost on an unsuccessful project? God is a God of restoration. The restoration process is not as easy as inserting a recovery CD and pressing run. It takes time, humility, planning and work for the restoration to take effect. But, God desires to restore your soul, your peace and your spirit so that you can be victorious daily. The psalmist, David, found himself in need of restoration after being on the run for his life from King Saul. He didn't know who to trust or where to turn. As a result and his life was in a chaotic state. The enemy desires for your life to stay in the "crashed" and disjointed state. But, let God restore your soul, your relationships and your spirit through His word and by His Spirit. The CD can restore the computer back to the default settings. God, however, can restore you to be better than before the crash. Let God restore your soul and make you better than whole again.

Prayer

Father, I thank you for daily restoring me in spite of the problems I face daily. Restore my strength, peace and determination to live the life you intended for me. In Jesus' name I pray. Amen.

Prayer Concerns

_____
_____
_____
_____
_____
_____
_____
_____
_____
_____
_____
_____
_____
_____
_____
_____
_____

Celebrate the God of Restoration.

Restoration

Journal/Reflect/Strategize

Restoration

He restoreth my soul: he leadeth me in the paths of righteousness for his name's sake. Psalm 23:3 (KJV)

Restore unto me the joy of thy salvation; and uphold me with thy free spirit. Psalm 51:12 (KJV)

And I will restore to you the years that the locust hath eaten, the cankerworm, and the caterpillar, and the palmerworm, my great army which I sent among you. Joel 2:25 (KJV)

Devotional Objective: God is the God of restoration. God wants you to be whole in every area of your life. God stands ready to walk us through the restoration process in our lives. Some of the process may be hard or require work but, the work will be worth the reward.

Materials Needed
Everyday Miracles Book
2 large or several small Rubik's Cubes™
Any toys or games that have to be put together
Everyday Miracles Music CD
Holy Bible (version of your choice)
Dictionary of choice
Worksheet – Restore1

Vocabulary
Restoration
Processing
Whole
Broken

Opening Activity: Open with prayer. Allow time for celebrations, announcements and prayer concerns. Read the devotional and prayer entitled, Restoration (Page 71 in the Everyday Miracles book), and write down any prayer concerns. (Music can be played during opening activity.) Share any thoughts regarding the scripture, devotional or prayer.

Questions for Consideration: Are there areas in your life that need to be restored? How do you think that these areas became broken? What part did you play, if any, with the broken areas? What can you do to help to restore these areas? What part does God have to play in the restoration process?

Activities:
Activity #1 - If using a large Rubik's Cube, show the entire group a whole or finished Rubik's cube. Then, show the entire group a scrambled or unfinished Rubik's cube. Ask the group if there is someone in the group that can complete the Rubik's cube back together whole like the untouched Rubik's cube. If there is a person in your group who can assemble the Rubik's Cube, allow them time to put it together. In the meantime, discuss the following questions:

Discussion/Share: What do you think it takes to put the Rubik's cube together? Do you feel that it would be hard or easy to figure out the key to restoring the Rubik's cube? Why do some people give up on working the Rubik's cube?

Activity #1 Alternate - If you are using smaller Rubik's cubes, give out one Rubik's Cube to several members of the group and ask them to solve the puzzle back to the original cube.

Note: Realize that the Rubik's Cube will not be restored or solved on its own. You have to pick up the Rubik's Cube and work it to solve it. If restoration is to take place in us we be a participant. What is your role in restoration?

Respond/Share/Journal
Respond: Each group member should have a copy of Worksheet Restore1 and have time to complete.

Share: After a period of time, let group members share their thoughts with the entire group or with a partner with the group. (Note: people do not have to share their personal issues unless they feel comfortable. If there are no group members who want to share, discuss about the restoration process instead)

Journal: Play a song from the Everyday Miracles Music CD and give time for journaling about Restoration. (Note: If someone has difficulty with things to journal about, feel free to ask the questions to guide discussion.) What are the next steps in your restoration process?

Closing activity, thoughts and prayer
Closing Thoughts and Prayer: Restoration is a two way process. There is someone who has to be the initiator of the process and someone who has to be the receiver. In any case, there must be a beginning. There may be people that you have to forgive or others you may have to ask forgiveness. The restoration process requires humility and effort. Restoration will not happen on its own. Are you willing to be the initiator of the process or will you leave issues broken? Pray that each group member will be strengthened, guided and assured that God has chosen and will equip them.

Extension Activity: What's next? If you have a relationship that needs to be restored, who do you need to call or meet? If you have a career that needs to be restored, where and when do you start school or receive some additional training to advance? If it's your health that needs to be restored, have you made a doctor's appointment? If your money needs to be restored, do you have all of your financial records and when are you meeting with a financial adviser?

Follow-up Activity and Resources
- Read the next or assigned devotional prior to the next meeting time
- Listen to music provided on the Everyday Miracles music CDs
- Read: Genesis 40; Ruth 4:15; Psalm 23:3; Jeremiah 30:17; Joel 2:25
- At the next meeting, allow opportunity for sharing and or testimony as a follow-up on their progress of the "Restoration" Lesson.

God wants every area of your life whole and not broken. He is willing to restore any broken areas of your life. Evaluate the following areas of your life. Are there some things that you should change?

Health

Relationships

Career

Spiritual Growth

Finances

What steps do you need to take to restore any broken areas of your life?

Worksheet—Restore1

Seasons

What Season Are You in Right Now?

"The eyes of all wait upon thee; and thou givest them their meat in due season."
Psalm 145:15 (KJV)

Seasons

Spring brings flowers, birds and thawing of the ground to prepare for sowing. Summer has the overwhelming heat, sun and work to prepare for harvest. Fall, in recent years, has been plagued with hurricanes, thunder storms, cyclones and unusual climatic temperature swings. Winter brings ice, snow and dangerous conditions that leave us praying for spring again. In what season of life are you? Are you in the spring of bloom and growth? Are you experiencing the heat of summer with trials, tribulations and turmoil? Do you feel the brisk fall winds blowing, signaling a change of season and the unexpected? Or, do you feel that your life is frozen solid in time like winter? God created the seasons. He knows everything that you are going through and why. Ask God for his help, guidance and direction. There is a reason for every season. Whether you find yourself in the season of winter, spring, summer or fall, remember God is a God for all seasons.

Prayer

Lord, I thank you that you are my help in each season of my life. I ask that you guide, energize and provide for people around the world. Show yourself strong in each of our lives. In Jesus' name I pray. Amen.

Prayer Concerns

What is the current season in your life?

Seasons

Journal/Reflect/Strategize

There is a time for everything, and a season for every activity under heaven:
Ecclesiastes 3:1 (NIV)

Devotional Objective: Whatever Season you find yourself, God is right there to guide you and help you to live a victorious life.

Materials Needed
Everyday Miracles Book
Everyday Miracles Music CD
Holy Bible (version of your choice)
Worksheet Season1
Worksheet Season2
Dictionary of choice
(Suggestion: Prepare a snack or treat that would be served in the current season of your study. For example, if it is summer, have popsicles or lemonade. If it is winter, prepare hot chocolate, etc.)

Vocabulary
Season
Time
Period

Opening Activity: Allow time for celebrations, announcements and prayer concerns. Read the devotional and prayer entitled, Seasons (Page 75 in the Everyday Miracles book), and write down any prayer concerns. (Music can be played during opening activity.) Share any thoughts regarding the scripture, devotional or prayer.

Questions for discussion: What is your favorite season and what is your least favorite season? What would be the result of not having these seasons throughout the year? Currently, does your life feel like one of these seasons? Which one and why?

Activities:
Activity #1: Every group member should have a copy of Worksheet Season1. Ask each group member to independently describe each season of the year. As a group, review the characteristics of each season. Ask each group member to determine which season describes their everyday life.

Share/Discussion: Allow group members to discuss the seasons and why they feel that their natural or spiritual life is in a particular season.

Activity #2: Every group member should have a copy of Worksheet Season2. On Worksheet Season2, each group member should write coping activities they use to get through each season of the year.

Share/Discussion: As a group, review the coping techniques of each season. Allow group members to discuss the coping techniques of each season. Ask the group how they can use the coping techniques for the natural seasons and transfer it to their spiritual life.

Respond/Share/Journal

Respond: After completing the two activities, which season would you prefer? Why?

Share: Allow time to share responses in a small or large group.

Journal: Play a song from the Everyday Miracles Music CD and give time for journaling about the Seasons lesson. (Note: If someone has difficulty with things to journal about, feel free to ask the questions to guide discussion.)

Closing activity, thoughts and prayer

Closing Thoughts and Prayer: God created each natural season. He is orchestrating each season of your spiritual life as well. No matter what season you find yourself in, ask God for help and obey His voice. Pray over every person in the group for guidance, peace and comfort to make it through each season of their life. Pray that each group member will be strengthened, guided and assured that God has chosen and will equip them.

Follow-up Activity and Resources

- Read the next or assigned devotional prior to the next meeting time.
- Listen to music provided on the Everyday Miracles music CDs.
- Read: Genesis 1:14; Ecclesiastes 3; Jeremiah 5:24; Daniel 2:21; Galatians 4:10.
- At the next meeting, allow opportunity for sharing and or testimony as a follow-up on their progress of the "Seasons" Lesson.

Seasons

Currently, what season are you in? In the space provided, write descriptive words for each season of the year.

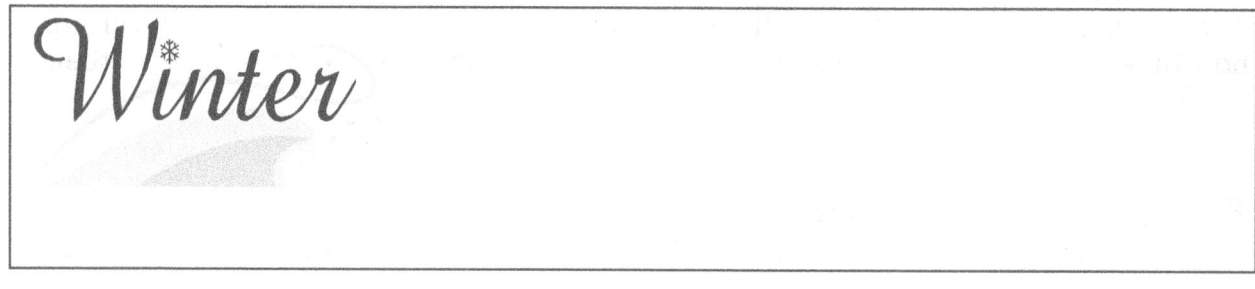

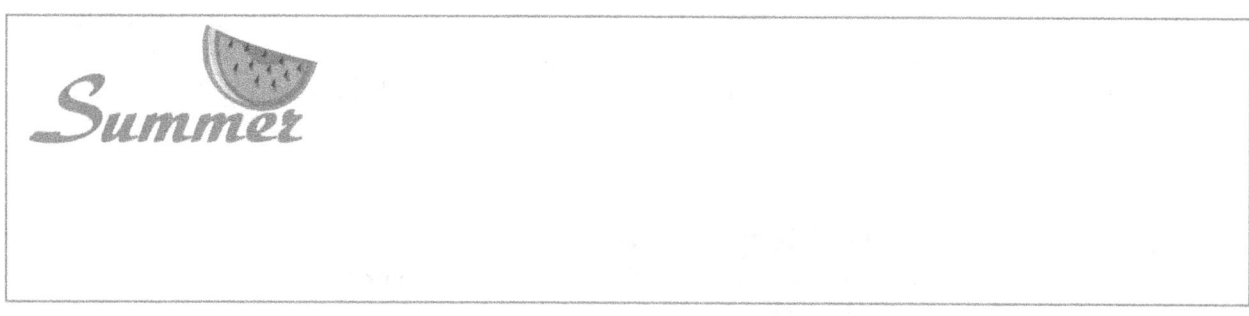

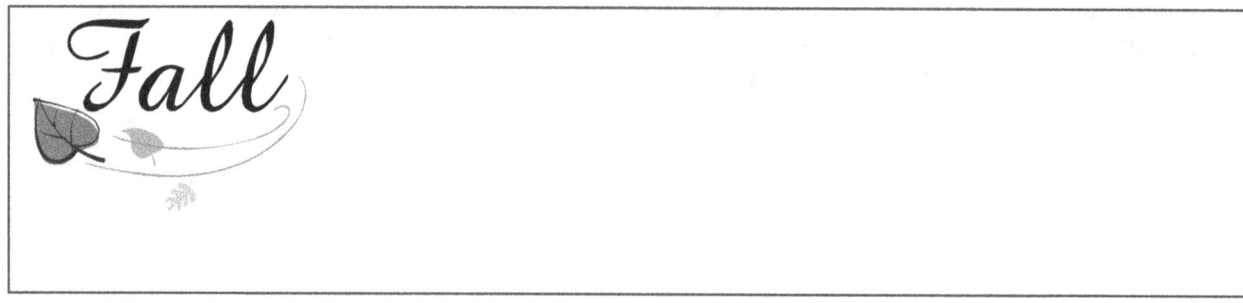

Worksheet—Seasons 1

Seasons

What are your coping techniques for each season?

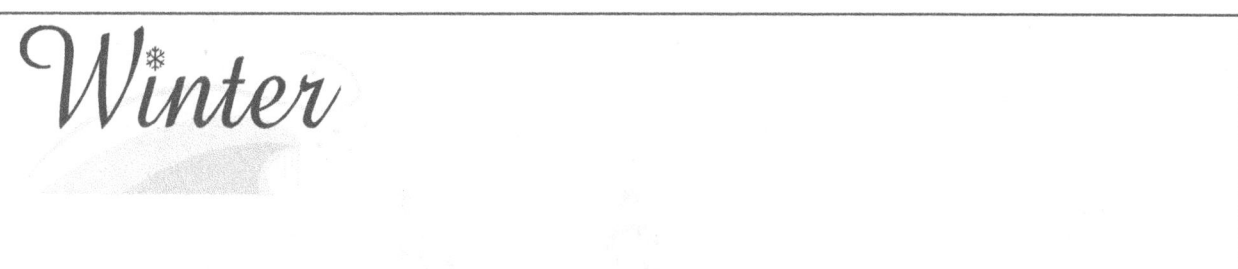

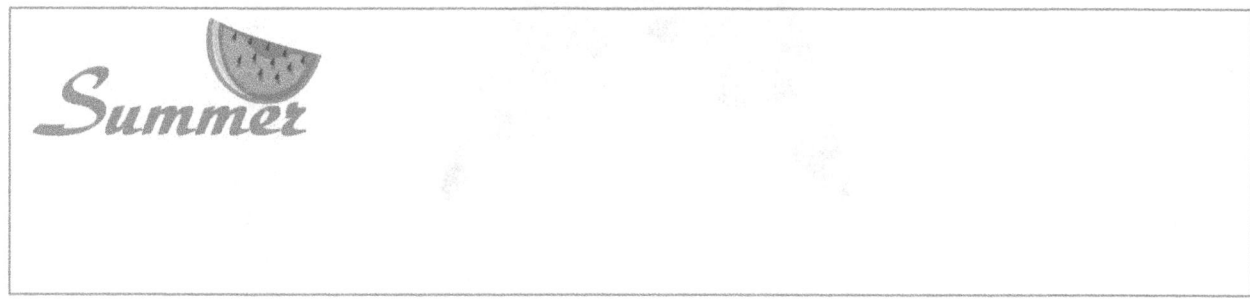

Worksheet—Seasons2

Tug Boat or Row Boat

Which Boat are You?

"And the God of all grace, who called you to his eternal glory in Christ, after you have suffered a little while, will himself restore you and make you strong, firm and steadfast." I Peter 5:10(KJV)

Tug boat or Row boat?

Each day I cross the Ohio River to go to work. I noticed the many barges that move easily down the river. Pushing these barges is a tug boat. The barges contain coal, sand or other materials to their destination up or down river. At times, there are 4, 6 or 8 barges being pushed by one tug boat. The tug boats are designed to help businesses move essential merchandise along the river rather than by truck or train. A row boat on the other hand is found on the river as well but, in more shallow areas and is primarily used for entertainment or pleasure on a warm spring or summer day. There is no merchandise or cargo that can be handled by a row boat. A row boat is not designed to carry more than 2-4 people depending on its size and a picnic basket or smaller cooler. Spiritually, are you a tug boat or a row boat? Like the tugboat, do you experience the heavy weight of life? Are you still able to move through the rough waters by His spirit, guidance and power? Or are you spiritually like the row boat and only able to handle the smooth waters and pleasant times in life?

God is looking for people to carry out and fulfill His Kingdom purpose in the earth. Can He count on you? Are you a spiritual tug boat and ready to push forth the Lord's will for your life? Or are you a spiritual row boat waiting on God to deliver the next blessing? Look at the river of your life and decide whether you want to be a row boat or a tug boat.

Prayer

Father we thank you for your strength that you give us each day to bear the burdens of this life. Help us to continue to be a spiritual tugboat and not a spiritual row boat. We shall be forever grateful. In Jesus' name. Amen.

Prayer Concerns

Are you a tug boat or a row boat?

Tug boat or Row boat?

Journal/Reflect/Strategize

Tugboat or a Rowboat

Until we all reach unity in the faith and in the knowledge of the Son of God and become mature, attaining to the whole measure of the fullness of Christ. Ephesians 4:13 (NIV)

Perseverance must finish its work so that you may be mature and complete, not lacking anything. James 1:4 (NIV)

Devotional Objective: The importance of spiritual maturity to move forward with the work of the Kingdom.

Materials Needed
Everyday Miracles Book
Everyday Miracles Music CD
Visit www.encyclopedia.com and obtain facts about tugboats and row boats.
A toy version of a tug boat and/or row boat for demonstration.
Several Popular Magazines that can be cut up
Holy Bible (version of your choice)
Worksheet Tug1
Worksheet Tug2
Dictionary of choice

Vocabulary
Maturity
Strength
Growth

Opening Activity: Allow time for celebrations, announcements and prayer concerns. Read the devotional and prayer entitled, Tug boat or Row boat (Page 79 in the Everyday Miracles book), and write down any prayer concerns. (Music can be played during opening activity.) Share any thoughts regarding the scripture, devotional or prayer.

    Questions for Discussion: Do you characterize yourself as a tugboat or rowboat? Do others agree with your self assessment?

Activities:
    Activity #1: If you have the toy tug boat or row boat, display the two toys and begin discussion about the difference in the two boats. Each group member should have and complete Worksheet Tug1. If little is known about tug boats or row boats, review your findings from encyclopedia.com website.

Discussion: Is there any resemblance to the work that these vessels do in your life?

Activity #2: Each group member should have access to scissors, glue, popular magazines and the Worksheet Tug2. Group members can work in groups or individually to complete Worksheet Tug2.

Share: Allow time for individuals to share their findings with the group or journal their response later in the session.

Respond/Share/Journal

Respond: After completing these two activities, how do you see tug boats or row boats differently? Are you a tug boat or a row boat?

Share: Each group member can be allowed time to complete both worksheets. Allow time to for individuals to share in a small group or to the large group either Worksheet Tug1 or Tug2.

Journal: Play a song from the Everyday Miracles Music CD and give time for journaling about the Tugboat or Rowboat lesson. (Note: If someone has difficulty with the journal portion, feel free to refer to the questions to guide discussion.)

Closing activity, thoughts and prayer:

Closing thoughts and prayer: God is with us whether we are experiencing difficult or good times in our lives. We may feel overwhelmed with the cares of this life. In fact you may feel that you are pulling more weight than you think you deserve. God is there to strengthen, guide and empower you through any situation. God is the ultimate vessel that will navigate you through the turbulent waters of life. Pray that each group member will be strengthened, guided and assured that God has chosen and will equip them.

Follow-up Activity and Resources

- Read the next or assigned devotional prior to the next meeting time.
- Listen to music provided on the Everyday Miracles music CD
- Read Mark 4:35-41
- At the next meeting, allow time for sharing a testimony regarding progress made as a follow-up to the Tug Boat or Row Boat lesson.

Tug Boat or Row Boat

What are the characteristics of each boat? Next to each boat, write down some words that describe these two boats.

Do you see any of these characteristics in your own life? Are there characteristics that you possess that you wish that you didn't? Are there other characteristics that you are striving to incorporate in your life?

Worksheet—Tug1

Tug Boat or Row Boat

Worksheet—Tug2

You are a Miracle!

Look in the Mirror, What Do You See?

"I will praise thee; for I am fearfully and wonderfully made: marvellous are thy works." Psalm 139:14 (KJV)

"Then God said, Let us make man in our image, in our likeness, and let them rule." Genesis 1:26 (KJV)

You are a Miracle

No matter what has been said about, to or over you, God says that He loves you. You are made in God's image and His likeness. He thinks you're exquisite. He created you by looking at a mirror of Himself. He said, "let us make man in our image, in our likeness…" He knew all about your imperfections, personality traits and sometimes, wrong tendencies but, nothing you do can stop Him from loving you. He still loved you so much He died for you. He thinks you are special. He told Jeremiah and tells you as well, that before you were formed in your mother's womb, He knew you. Secondly, He knew all what you could, couldn't and wouldn't do but, he still set you apart from the others or sanctified you. Furthermore, He ordained you, which means; He placed His hand of anointing on you, gave you a position and told the whole world about it. You are God's creation, fearfully and wonderfully made to grow, rule and live the abundant life. With this knowledge, we give worship to God with thanksgiving, reverence and praise. This knowledge is not to be exalted or conceited but, to give praise to God for the miracle of life placed inside of you. Get your own mirror and look closely because a miracle is you.

Prayer

Thank you God for creating me in your image and likeness. Help my life to be a reflection of your glory in the earth. In Jesus' name I pray. Amen.

Prayer Concerns

_____
_____
_____
_____
_____
_____
_____
_____
_____
_____
_____
_____
_____
_____
_____

You are a miracle. Thank God for you!

You are a Miracle

Journal/Reflect/Strategize

You are a Miracle!

"If you put a small value on yourself, rest assured that the world will not raise your price."
Author Unknown

To love him with all your heart, with all your understanding and with all your strength, and to love your neighbor as yourself is more important than all burnt offerings and sacrifices.
Mark 12:23 (KJV)

Devotional Objective: To advocate a healthy self image and self-love.

Materials Needed
Everyday Miracles Book
Everyday Miracles Music CD
Several small mirrors
Holy Bible (version of your choice)
Worksheet You1 and You2
Dictionary of choice

Vocabulary
Esteem
Image

Opening Activity: Allow time for celebrations, announcements and prayer concerns. Read the devotional and prayer entitled, "You are a Miracle" (Page 83 in the Everyday Miracles book), and write down any prayer concerns. (Music can be played during opening activity.) Share any thoughts regarding the scripture, devotional or prayer.

    Questions for Consideration: When you look in the mirror, what do you see and what do you say? When you are dressed up for church or a special event, what is the first thing that you say to yourself?

Activities:
    Activity #1: Each group member should have a small mirror and Worksheet You1. For a few minutes, ask every person to look in a mirror at themselves. Each group member should complete Worksheet You1.
    Discussion: What do you see when you look in the mirror?

Share: Allow time for individuals to share their thoughts to a small or the entire large group.

Activity #2: Each group member should complete Worksheet You2.
Discussion/Share: Allow time for individuals to share their thoughts to a small or the entire large group.

Respond/Share/Journal
Respond: After completing both activities, do you feel differently about yourself? What do you need to say or do to have a more positive self-image?
Share: Allow time for individuals to share their thoughts to a small or the entire large group.
Journal: Play the song "Love Yourself" from the Everyday Miracles Music CD and give time for journaling about the "You are Miracle" lesson. (Note: If someone has difficulty with things to journal about, feel free to ask the questions to guide discussion.)

Closing activity, thoughts and prayer:
Closing thoughts and prayer: You are God's handiwork. God formed you in your mother's womb. No matter what the situation you were born into, you are God's miracle. He has a plan for your life. He designed you with a purpose. He created you with a gift. He will do great things through you if you follow Him. Pray that each group member will be strengthened, guided and assured that God has chosen and will equip them.

Extension Activity: For the next thirty days, repeat one affirmation from Worksheet You1. Partner with one person in the group. Send them a personal note or email about how special they are to God and you.

Follow-up Activity and Resources
- Listen to music provided on the Everyday Miracles music CDs.
- Read: John 3:16; Jeremiah 1:4-19; Psalm 139
- If this is the final lesson for your group study, plan and prepare a celebration for group members and other invited guests.

Personal Affirmation

Write down 10 positive things about yourself.

Turn to another person in the group and list 3 positive things about them.

Worksheet—You1

You are a Miracle!

Write 5 or more scriptures that refer to God's Love toward humanity.

How does God feel about you? How does God see you? Does that change how you feel about you knowing how God feels about you?

Worksheet—You2

r's Guide the
cles book and
s Instructor's
assist instructors
e an enjoyable
study. The Eve-
e contains the
ences, Activity
abulary, Exten-
d printable
e intent of the
Guide, is to en-
t and eyes are
g miracles daily.

uthor, motivational
o her credit, she has
authored 3 Books,
sletter "A Jar in the
urage, enlighten and
ndant life, Julia is a
d to Brian K. Roys-
ia, visit

ISBN 978-0-9818135-4-7
52000
9 780981 813547

en

A Devotional, W

INSTRUCT

BY JULIA